# LIVING
# DHARMA

## THE FLAVOUR OF LIBERATION
## VOLUME 4

### BURGS

# OTHER BOOKS BY THE AUTHOR

We would like to thank everyone who has contributed to the editing and compiling of this book.

# ABOUT THE AUTHOR

Originally from the UK, Burgs began his meditation practice in Asia, initially as an assistant for the famous Indonesian healer and meditation teacher Merta Ada. He went on to practise meditation under the guidance of some of the greatest living Buddhist meditation masters, with HH Dodrupchen Rinpoche and Pa Auk Sayadaw as his principal teachers. He spent many years doing intensive self-practice under the guidance of his teachers in both India and Burma where he ordained as a monk, to be personally tutored and trained by Pa Auk Sayadaw. On completion of his training, during which he practised to the highest levels of Jhana concentration, he disrobed in order to bring what he had learned to a Western audience within the context of a lay life. He was recognised by his teachers as having unusual depth of practice and ability and began teaching at their request.

He first held retreat in 1996 and has since hosted over a hundred retreats, from 5 days to 5 months in length, and has taught thousands of people from all walks of life. His students have ranged from total beginners, to distinguished monks and nuns; from the homeless of Asia, to some of Europe's most successful and influential businesspeople.

He has a rare ability to communicate deep knowledge of meditation and the mechanics and functioning of consciousness with a clarity that has been greatly appreciated by Western audiences, making him an extremely accessible teacher. Today he is one of the most experienced and accomplished meditation teachers in the West.

For further information about Burgs
and The Art of Meditation
please visit theartofmeditation.org

# ABOUT THIS BOOK

The book is structured according to the way the Buddha taught his Four Noble Truths, which frames the logic and intelligence of the content as it progresses.

Throughout the book we have maintained the style of Burgs' spoken word, using his contemporary anecdotes, which serve to extrapolate deep and subtle principles into easily understandable points, demystifying these precious teachings and allowing the reader to see these truths for themselves within their own experience.

Most of the content of the book is taken from live discourses delivered by Burgs to various audiences engaged in intensive meditation retreats: as such, we have endeavoured to maintain the flavour and essence of the spoken word in his original delivery. It is our hope that in doing so we have maintained as much of the transmission conveyed at the time as possible. This accounts for some of the repetition within the book, which we hope serves to reiterate the subtleties and nuances within the teachings themselves. We strongly recommend that the reader takes time to listen to some of the original recordings on which the text is based.

It is not necessary to have read 'The Flavour of Liberation' Volumes 1, 2 or 3 to benefit from or understand the content presented in this book.

# CONTENTS

# PART IV

The Fourth Noble Truth: The Path That Leads To The Cessation Of Suffering

From Bondage To Freedom—The Journey Home

# PART I

———— ◆ ————

## THE FIRST NOBLE TRUTH: THE TRUTH OF SUFFERING

——————

## THE APPEARANCE OF THINGS — IS LIFE REALLY SUFFERING?

# CHAPTER ONE

# TWENTY-FIVE CENTURIES ON: A LIVING DHARMA

Reflecting upon the direction of his life and the nature of suffering, the Buddha looked out at the world from his life of privilege and luxury over twenty-five centuries ago, and in spite of having everything a young man could possibly dream of, he felt a sense of dismay arise within him. He made the reflection that this life is fraught with danger, and humans are inclined to bring themselves to suffering, even when they are blessed with the highest of good fortune.

This was not a man experiencing hardship and misfortune. He was a young prince, physically strong and virile, with all of life's pleasures to hand. He was not bemoaning his lot when he made the reflection that this life is suffering, he was simply witnessing the deep and ingrained tendency human beings have to bring suffering to themselves and others. And in witnessing this fact, he was so moved by it that he set forth from his life of privilege in search of a way to the cessation of suffering.

The realisations that he came to in his epic and heroic quest for the cessation of suffering, and the path that he taught that leads to that goal, have, over the centuries that followed, become one of the most profound and widely followed sets of spiritual teachings in all of history. Beyond being simply a philosophical system, it has for countless generations pointed a way that others have embarked upon and lived by. Over time it has led all of those who have completed this path not only to reach the same realisation as the Buddha did, but to experience for themselves the cessation of suffering.

The Buddha's appearance in the world, although of enormous significance, didn't change the way of things. Today, two and a half millennia later, it is still the same world that we live in. Folk are still prone to create suffering for themselves and others, and the route by which this suffering comes to an end remains the same.

Dharma is a word from the ancient Sanskrit language of India which means truth, or 'way of things.' It does not refer to a philosophical system but is instead an expression of living principles governing life. The Buddha's realisation of the cessation of suffering marks nothing more than the coming into alignment with, and the gradual ending of conflict with, these principles that govern our lives. When we look out at the world today we can see now, as has always been the case, this living Dharma expressing itself in all things, everywhere.

The Dharma has encountered both support and scrutiny over the time that has followed the Buddha's eighty years upon this earth. But the

Dharma is a living truth, it is there to be seen in the world around us, in each and every moment. If we are to understand the Dharma, we have to do as the Buddha did and look to the world, and us its inhabitants, to observe its workings and see for ourselves the path that leads out of suffering.

This book has been called Living Dharma for that very reason. The Dharma is alive, it is within us, and within all things, always and everywhere. It is just waiting for us to clear the dust from our eyes so that we might see it. The Buddha claimed that one who sees life as it is will see the Dharma, and one who sees the Dharma will see life as it is.

The Buddha's Four Noble Truths are not complex and hard to grasp. Together they explain the underlying intelligence behind life, the processes and conditions by which it expresses itself as suffering, the conditions under which that suffering comes to an end, and the process by which those conditions for the cessation of suffering gradually come about. Intellectually we can all make sense of them. For as long as there is no end to what we would do in the pursuit of our desires, then there is no end to the suffering we would create in that pursuit.

Knowledge alone may prompt us to reflect, and sometimes deeply so, but those deeply instinctual drives of ours, as well as the ones we have inherited and developed for ourselves, have a powerful and inexorable pull to them. Turning them around to the point where there would no longer be a willingness to harm either ourselves or others in the pursuit of such desires will take more tenacity, humility and determination than we might initially feel we want to put forth.

But we are, in the final analysis, still the most intelligent form of life on this planet. While blessed with the capacity to bend it to our will, we likewise have the capacity to recognise when this is no longer appropriate, acceptable or even possible. We live in the same world, governed by the same natural laws, as the one the Buddha looked out upon.

His world was not in nearly as much peril as the one we today look out upon. He himself said that the Dharma would only flourish for as long as we do not become so blinded by dust in our eyes that we cannot see the truth when we look upon it, nor hear it when it is spoken.

The Buddha said that there are four types of beings on this planet. There are those in the darkness moving towards the darkness, and there are those in the darkness moving towards the light. There are those in the light moving towards the darkness, and there are those in the light moving towards the light. What he was saying is that, good fortune or misfortune notwithstanding, the only thing that really matters is the direction that we are heading in from where we are now.

So what direction are we heading in? It is an important question to be asking ourselves now. There is an intelligence within all of us that is capable of making sense of our predicament. At that level, it is plain to see that for all the physical hardship that exists in this world, there are countless unfortunate folk who, although challenged, meet their challenges daily and find grace within their lives. Equally, there are countless fortunate folk who, blessed with the most extraordinary good fortune, are still deeply miserable and dissatisfied. It is clearly the case that it is not so much what we experience in life that determines our happiness, but how we meet it.

We are all intelligent enough to see what is happening to us if we are willing to pay a little attention. But our welfare in the future will not be built on understanding alone, it will be built on conduct and choices. There is a storm blowing upon the world and there is much dust in the air. Perhaps it is time for us to revisit the wisdom that the Buddha shared with us and see if we can understand, each of us, what it was he was really trying to tell us.

This book is offered not as a social commentary but as a reflection upon how the living Dharma is expressed and displayed in our lives, so that we might take the liberating wisdom of the Buddha off the page and into our hearts and use it as a road map for our own way home.

# CHAPTER TWO

# WAS THE BUDDHA RIGHT, IS LIFE JUST SUFFERING?

S o why do we find life hard? Why do we find it such a struggle? Twenty-five centuries ago the Buddha made an assertion: 'Truly this life is suffering.' He had searched for, found, and experienced every sensual peak experience there was to be had and every possible expression of good fortune that could come one's way. He was born a prince, growing up in the most extraordinary environment, never wanting for anything, never sick, indulging in the most exquisite of sensual pleasures, and yet he still came to the conclusion: 'Truly this life is suffering.' Why do you think he did that? He was the most exalted and fortunate human being you could possibly imagine and so we would think he was in a position to easily avoid suffering.

There are things involved in being alive in this human body, exquisite and extraordinary though it is, that are suffering. Getting sick, growing old and dying; that is suffering. Not getting what you want; that is suffering. Getting what you do not want; that is suffering. Or is it? How much of life is actually suffering and how much do we turn it into suffering?

He went out in search of the end of all suffering, having had the pinnacle of all sensual pleasures, the peak of sensual experiences and indulgences. There was nothing left for him to dine on that would have been more exquisite than the things he had already experienced. He left behind the material and sensual experiences of pleasure in search of something else. And in his pursuit of the cessation of suffering he pursued all kinds of spiritual practices.

He pursued the yogic practices of the age to the very highest levels of concentration practice, the most profound experiences of peace and serenity that the human consciousness is capable of experiencing. There was not a peak experience that the Buddha did not experience and then he reflected: 'No matter how awesome, extraordinary and amazing these experiences are, they do not last forever, and if I long for them when I do not have them, I am left with a feeling of tremendous lacking.'

So he gave up all sensual indulgences, including the pursuit of the peak pleasures of mind that come about through deep meditative practices, such as the meditative pleasures of bliss, rapture and joy, and the profound states of serenity which had surpassed all the material and sensual pleasures he had experienced.

Yet he still came to the conclusion: 'Despite all this, I'm left facing old age, sickness and death. There is no guarantee whether or not I can attain these levels of pleasure; they are unreliable; they are not the end of suffering, even if momentarily, while I am experiencing them, I am completely free from suffering.'

What he realised was that he had taken refuge in the pleasurable, and the pursuit of it, and came to understand that he could not guarantee that he would always find the pleasurable or be able to surround himself with it.

We do not know when misfortune is going to come our way. We do not know when we are not going to be able to get the things for which we long. The Buddha realised that those sensual pleasures to which he had grown accustomed could one day have been stripped away, that one day he may not have had access to them, and then what?

With this reflection, having left his royal palace and gone off in search of whatever peak experiences remained through the practices of concentration and meditation, he rejected them all and he strove on. He lived as an ascetic in the forest for six years, looking for what he called the causal cessation of suffering: the state, condition or place, or whatever it may be, where suffering ceases to arise.

He tried all kinds of things: he tried to stop breathing, he shut his senses down so he could not feel anything anymore, he stopped himself from thinking, he starved himself, and he very nearly died. He lived in a forest with five other ascetics, all ardently practising the most austere yogic practices of the time, and yet, nothing, no breakthrough emerged. He was almost dead from exhaustion, not eating enough and pushing himself too hard. This glorious human being who once was the most handsome of princes, desired by all the damsels of the day, was now a waif by the side of a river, skin hanging off him, almost dead.

Then one day a maiden from the nearby village came down to wash dishes in the river that he was bathing in and saw this pitiful creature. Yet she saw this diamond-like shining in his eyes, frail though he was and close to death, and she took pity on him. She went and she made him delicious, sweet rice pudding, and she took it back and begged him, 'Please eat this!' He had hardly been eating anything for a long time, a few grains, nuts, seeds and he was wasted.

He saw in her eyes the compassion that she felt for him and he took the rice and ate it, and it fortified him. And he made the reflection, 'These two extremes that I have pursued: this extreme pursuit of pleasure and sensual indulgence never satisfied me, always left me wanting more, but these austere practices that I pursued to cut off at the sense doors all capacity to experience suffering, I still struggle to forbear the aches and pains of my body. I get exhausted, I need to sleep at night, it is painful to sleep on the dirt. I am racked with pain, I am exhausted, I can hardly walk. This too most definitely is not the causal cessation of suffering.'

So he gave it all up, and he left the five ascetics that he had been with in the forest. And when they saw him eating this sweet rice pudding they thought, 'Oh Siddhartha, he's become soft, he's given up!' And they all rejected him, turned their backs on him and walked away and left him.

So there he was on his own, on the May full-moon night, when he made a strong determination; he sat under a tree and said to himself, 'I am going to free myself from suffering and its causes this very night or I shall die trying. I shall sit here and I shall cross my legs and I shall cross my arms and I shall close my eyes and I shall not cease until either death comes upon me or I free myself from suffering.'

That night he brought to bear all the training that he had received as a yogi. He had been taught by the greatest masters of India, and he had attained more swiftly than they had the highest levels of samādhi and meditation. On that night he worked his way through these attainments until his mind was supremely bright and clear. Emerging from samādhi and its deeply peaceful state, he reviewed this body, looking through it to see what it was and how it was the way it was.

To understand how the Buddha was able to perceive so clearly the intricate workings of the body and mind, we have to understand what happens to our faculty of perception when we enter into a profoundly concentrated and focused state. Our ordinary conscious mind perceives only around ten per cent of reality. Our ordinary bandwidth of perception is quite limited and narrow, and we tend to be fixated upon the physical appearance of things. Even when we concentrate, with an ordinary level of mental focus, it is only like looking at things through a magnifying glass. There is no significant increase in the depth of our perception.

But once we become deeply concentrated, the mind gradually becomes able to perceive the multilayered nature of reality with ever more clarity. Not only does the lens of our mind become more akin to a microscope, but the subtle material and energetic fields of reality gradually come into focus, revealing more of the multidimensional nature of reality.

In such a way, the Buddha was able to look beyond the veiled appearance of things and glimpse the causal or creative process at work in the background. One of the most significant realisations we come to when we do learn to perceive reality at this level is that this is a conscious universe out of which material phenomena are arising. This is in opposition to our tendency to assume that the universe consists of material phenomena within which consciousness is an occasionally arising by-product.

He reviewed what were the causes for the arising of the body and material states, the causes for its passing away and why it was so prone to suffering. And then he reviewed the mind, having reviewed the body. In doing so he saw how the body arises dependent upon the mind. It was while reviewing this that he came to see that consciousness is the primal cause for the arising of materiality and not the other way round. He saw that in the absence of consciousness new material states do not come into being.

He watched the mind arise and pass away, he watched the cause for its arising and passing away and the cause for the arising of affliction, both mental and physical. Then he reviewed the causal process, the creative process by which this life comes into being. He reviewed it with this eye of wisdom, a supremely concentrated mind that is utterly focused and undisturbed. Free of any mental elaboration and the tendency to formulate ideas, he was able to observe the true nature of these things and see them for what they are in their nakedness.

He reviewed what were the causes of this perception of suffering. Obviously there is that suffering that is caused by physical affliction alone, but beyond that there is mental suffering. In fact, most of our suffering is mental suffering. It is the experience of not being able to bear or be with the experience we are having in some way.

Now let us be clear about what we mean: suffering is to not be happy. Happiness is to be free of mental suffering. Happiness is contentment. Suffering is discontentment.

What the Buddha realised was that this suffering is not brought to an end through the pursuit of pleasure. The desire for pleasurable indulgences leaves us only with desire, to the point that when we fulfil our desires, we are left only with a sense of lacking something to desire.

This desire chases its tail, it never ends and it is never satisfied. Its very nature is to need.

He realised that the chasing after sensual pleasures never satisfied itself and this could have raged on until he had consumed everything that was available to him, until nothing was left, and he knew he would never have been happy. He realised that it is not these pleasant or unpleasant experiences themselves that cause us suffering, although the experience of pain is an affliction. The real suffering is our inability to be with what is. He realised that it was clinging, that it was grasping, that it was trying to hold onto or reject an experience that is in a process of constant change, of constant arising and passing away – it is that which is the cause of our suffering.

He reflected, 'I never appreciated any of these extraordinary things that came my way because I always wanted more. What if I were to just appreciate the exquisite for what it is and allow things to pass away as is their nature, without clinging to them? Then these things would not be the cause of any suffering in me. If while I was sick, full of fever and close to death I had realised that this is the momentary affliction of a body that is out of balance, and not rejected that experience, not worried about what was going to happen to me, fraught with fear and loathing, I would not have experienced a proliferation of suffering in my mind. What if I had just realised that this is what happens, that sickness is a part of life, but it does not last forever, that everything changes? If I had been with those experiences, both pleasurable and displeasurable, without grasping or rejecting them, they would not have caused me mental suffering.'

So he came to the understanding that it is the quality of mind with which we meet our experiences that is the cause of our suffering, not the experience itself. We create in our own minds our own misery through not being able to be with things as they are.

Happiness is not just a mental experience, it is a deeply embodied one; a 'sense' of happiness, a 'feeling' of happiness. Joy arises in us under certain circumstances and only under certain circumstances. It does not arise in our mind when we get what we have been longing for, strange though it may seem. After a brief moment of elation that may arise followed by the passing of it, the mind immediately looks around for something else to pursue. So the fulfilment of our desires does not equal happiness.

Happiness arises in the mind under one circumstance. When the heart is undisturbed by the experience we are having, a feeling of joy arises within us, a feeling of happiness spontaneously arises. It arises as a deeply felt experience. It arises directly in our awareness at a level that is beyond the thinking mind. This deeper aspect of awareness arises in the heart in a way that bypasses our analytical mind. This process the Buddha called direct perception, or direct knowing.

We can watch the arising of this sense of joy when we get really concentrated and equanimous and we are really able to rest deeply within ourselves, undisturbed by anything. We will witness this sense of happiness arising in the moment when our mind is not disturbing or smothering or grasping or rejecting our experience. This happens spontaneously and regardless of what it is that we are doing. It can arise while we are doing anything, even something as mundane as watching our breath.

If we watch, we will see a feeling of happiness arise in us when we are able to simply become absorbed in what we are doing. When we know that we can be totally with our experience without being disturbed in any way, the most extraordinary feeling of profound relief and joy arises within us, and these are the conditions under which real happiness arises.

There is no end to what humans have done in the pursuit of pleasure over the centuries, yet only a handful of beings die truly happy. There are few who end their lives deeply content, at peace and accepting of everything that has been. So our real challenge is not to orchestrate our lives so that we get all the things we want, but to open up completely to what is already there and allow it to be what it is without conflict. All of our mental suffering is at some level a result of either our efforts to grasp and cling to things, or our efforts to reject and deny them.

Mental suffering is to experience conflict through either grasping or rejecting our experience. Our suffering ends when our conflict ends, when we can accept things as they are. When we finally get to the place where we can be with our own suffering, the next thing that arises in us is a feeling of bliss. The profound relief that I am no longer in conflict with that, that 'I can be with this'. This is the cessation of suffering.

The cessation of suffering is not making sure that you always get what you want. Sometimes the very effort to do so is what brings us to suffering. There is no greater misery than the unbearable vexation that we experience when we have fought tooth and nail to make the world go our way, knowing that if we relax for a moment it may all fall apart. That is a great misery and vexation and certainly there is no peace to be had in such accomplishments.

So if you can find an inner stillness within you in the face of all things that come your way, a tremendous relief comes upon you, and out of that comes an inner joy. In a state where you can truly be with yourself without needing to add anything to the ordinary moment, you become a happy human being. And in that moment you realise, 'My needs are few. I can step lightly on this earth and not be too much of a nuisance to others anymore.'

Now, what happens to us when we actually get to the place where we know that we can be with what is? What happens when we stop all that grasping and rejecting of our various experiences? When the simple things in life that we took for granted suddenly become the source of profound gratitude. When a quiet moment with nothing in it is a blessing, instead of something that we would shrink from and seek to avoid. Then we start to be close to experiencing the cessation of suffering.

Something happens to us that changes everything. What we thought we had to do to please ourselves is gone. Instead of our life being this pot that we are desperately trying to fill at great expense to the world around us, we realise that our pot is something that is full to the brim. And now we can start to pour back in all kinds of directions the things that we have to give. It changes everything.

When we reach the place where we can be with each moment and everything in it completely, we realise, 'Wow, I'm alive! What could I possibly add to this that would make it more exquisite than it already is?' The answer is nothing. We have tried to add everything we could possibly think of but nothing yet has left us ultimately satisfied.

In that middle ground between the extremes, resting quietly within yourself, you find your peace and you realise it did not stand upon or depend upon anything else at all coming your way. You just had to find it within yourself to really turn up and recognise it.

This is why we learn to meditate and practise on a cushion with nothing else to do and no distractions, just us, on our own, making peace with ourselves and finding our own happiness within. So do not reject what arises within you because it is what it is, whether you like it or not. Somewhere down the line there is a cause for it being there.

When we reflect back over our life and all the things we could not be with, we realise that it was not these things that happened to us that were the cause of our suffering, it was the fact that we could not be with them, that we could not simply accept that it was what it was.

How does something that happened to us five, ten, twenty, thirty years ago possibly have the capacity to cause us suffering today? It does not. It has no capacity to cause us suffering. It is not causing us suffering. What is causing us suffering is how we continue to react to what we think happened to us, only that. We create our suffering in our mind, because we cannot be with the experiences that we have. They are not all going to be pleasant, but they are all going to pass. How wonderful is that?

There was the Buddha, starting out at the beginning of his life thinking that happiness was the consummation of all of his desires and the pinnacle of his dreams and finally getting everything he wanted. How exhausting that would have been even if he had succeeded in getting everything he wanted.

He realised that he did not have to cut everything off and reject everything and say, 'No, sensual pleasures, they are not to be tolerated!' He realised that you do not have to go off in search of anything. You just have to stop where you are right now and be completely with what is in front of you without being in conflict with it.

That is our challenge. That is actually why we learn to meditate. We sit there, cross-legged, it is uncomfortable, perhaps we have not done it before. We are not used to paying attention for so long, we are not used to being that still. We are not used to not being able to do what we want, to check our phone, go and have a coffee or seek other distractions.

First of all, overcoming our restlessness, overcoming our laziness, overcoming the feeling of, 'I can't be bothered to keep going', knocking off the rough edges of our mind until there is a willingness to do it. And out of that willingness to do it, we start to engage more completely in what we are doing. And as we engage more completely in what we are doing we become absorbed in it, and in that moment we lose or leave behind this nonsense that is our 'I-making extravaganza'.

Finally, and for the first time, we are free of this idea of ourself, the stories we tell ourselves about who we think we are, and all the effort we make to present ourselves to the world in a way that might be approved of. And instead of layering our experiences with this inordinately complex idea of ourself, we just get on with what we are doing. And in that moment, quite unexpectedly, not knowing where it came from, we find ourselves feeling more relaxed, more peaceful, more settled, more contented, happier than we have felt in a very long time – doing nothing. And that changes everything.

So instead of asking, 'What's in it for me? What else should I be doing?' we might ask, 'Can I be with what is in front of me now and can I find a joy in it?' That is the real question we need to be asking ourselves.

Learning to meditate is learning to be happy just to be. Just being here is so extraordinary if we can pay full attention to it, and being able to be with ourselves is such a relief. So learn to rest effortlessly and calmly within yourself in an ordinary moment and leave everything as it is. What a relief.

# CHAPTER THREE

# LIFE IS CONSCIOUSNESS, CONSCIOUSNESS IS LIFE

I f, as the Buddha said, suffering is caused by not paying attention, then we should start by looking at what we are not paying attention to. And for that let us start right at the beginning, or if you like, let us start with the biggest question of all.

What do we think life really is? It is going on around us everywhere, we are an expression of it ourselves, it is the basic and fundamental principle that governs our entire experience of being, and yet for all of humanity's ingenuity it still remains, to a large extent, the most unfathomable mystery.

Now I would say that instead of trying to reduce it down into its constituent parts and rob it of its exquisite mystery, we should allow it to be the very mystery that it is and start to acknowledge that perhaps there might be more to it than meets the eye. That perhaps there might be more intelligence behind it than we have assumed.

In many ways, in our failed attempts to understand it scientifically, we may well have robbed it of its very sacredness. If we can reconnect to it, it might prompt us to respect and honour it more than we currently do.

We have spent a long, long time trying to figure this world out through scientific observation. The problem scientists have faced since they tried to unravel life's great mystery is that all they had to observe was the apparent physically expressed form of it. We can only quantify that which we can discretely perceive to be there.

The problem with this is that there is one great big elephant in the room the moment we even start down this route. And that is that life itself is consciousness. Consciousness is life. It is consciousness that is the intelligent organising principle that galvanises life and brings it into expression. Any attempt to understand life in the absence of consciousness is going to fall short. We have continued to adopt the 18th Century Western Enlightenment view that the universe is a material occurrence that under certain circumstances brings forth life. But what if, in truth, it was a conscious universe that under certain circumstances brings forth matter and expresses itself as life when this consciousness and matter interact?

Taking a materialist approach to understand life is a bit like trying to understand your computer simply by looking at the hardware. When you take the actual physical thing apart and look inside, trying to fathom how on earth it does all the myriad things it does, there is no way that by looking at the constituent parts you are going to figure it out. That is because the real functionality of the computer is governed not by its hardware, but by its software. It is the flow and current of information that brings it to life. We, the human being, indeed any form of life, are exactly the same.

Consciousness is the software package that brings this mass of flesh and bones to life. And it is the absence of it that marks it as dead. It is as simple as that. The appearance of consciousness within a living organism produces a subtle electromagnetic current or field. In fact, all things that are alive are alive because of this subtle current that is produced by consciousness. It is this current that flows life through us, and the absence of it is death. It isn't produced by the food we eat or the air we breathe. It is produced by the consciousness that arises within us.

If you ever watch a plant with your naked eye it is extremely hard to recognise the point at which it goes from being alive to the point at which it is completely dead. In a human being it is much more obvious. There is a moment that marks the point of death. Although the body does not look very different with the naked eye, because there is the same body, it has profoundly changed at an unseen level. It has changed so profoundly, in fact, that it is now no longer capable of performing any functions whatsoever. In just the same way a computer is not capable of performing any functions in the absence of its software.

The mark, the sign of life in all things is the appearance of this subtle field: this very, very delicate charge, or electromagnetic field. Its presence within the organism marks it as alive. The absence of it marks it as dead. With the withdrawal of consciousness from the body during the dying process, that subtle electrical field fades. There is a point at which it is no longer able to support the heart and it stops beating, and thereafter a point where all activity, even that of the brain and nerves, likewise ceases.

That field of life is produced by one thing, and only by one thing. It is produced by the arising of consciousness within the organism, by awareness itself. I am not talking about the kind of active intelligence that is produced by our brain, I am talking about the basic ground of our very being, which is consciousness or awareness itself.

Nature expresses itself absolutely perfectly. It is a pure response to the conditions around it. The degree to which it is interfered with will always be shown in the way in which it expresses itself. Since we as humans are governed by the same principles as all life and all of nature, we would likewise express ourselves absolutely perfectly for as long as we are allowed to. There is nothing in nature that becomes dysfunctional or sick in anything like the way a human being does. That is because we are capable of interfering with the natural order of things that we live so disconnected from.

The main interfering factor producing incoherence in this human life, sadly, is our idea of ourselves, our active mind, our personal will, and our ability to impose that personal will upon the things around us. The mind, and the idea of ourselves that it expresses, seeks constantly to add or take something away from the experience we are having, and in so doing interferes with the experience.

But not only that, the mind interferes with the current of awareness within us that is actually having the experience. Now that is not to say that we should not be completely engaged in the life. But understand that it is consciousness that produced the life within you. The quality of it will determine the integrity with which that life is allowed to flow through us, or the degree to which it is impeded. That impedance itself is what we call ignorance, or lack of awareness. It is the lack of awareness that blocks the flow of life and energy through us.

And it is our active mind that is the interfering principle, which is why we have to be unconscious for a third of our life in order to function nicely for the two thirds that we are awake. Quite simply we go to sleep to get our conscious mind out of the way for long enough for our higher intelligence to put us back together again. Now that is quite an extraordinary thing.

In other words, this very faculty of our human mind that gives us the capacity to identify our sense of ourselves as a living organism, to register discretely and to be aware of our own life expressing itself through us, with a separate sense of ourselves, is the very thing that causes the expression of life within us to become compromised or impeded. It is the same mind that marks the human being as the most complex, intelligent and evolved form of life at one level, and that makes it the messiest form of life at another.

Because there is not anywhere else in nature where you will see this life principle interfered with anything like as much as it is within a human being. The untold number of ways in which the human organism degenerates in the course of its life, the ways in which atrophy occurs within its life, and the sickness and disease that appear – there is nothing else in nature that suffers anything like as much as we humans suffer whether as a result of physical degeneration and physical pain, or mental degeneration and mental pain. Apart from infectious diseases like viruses and bacteria or parasites, there are very few sicknesses or ways that life decays elsewhere in the natural world.

These days very few humans simply die of old age or reach the end of life and just die of natural causes because the organism is simply worn out. The life principle in the human being is the most interfered-with expression of life there is. So our challenge as humans is to rise to the extraordinary opportunity that we have, something that most other forms of life do not have to the same extent, which is to turn up consciously within our experience, becoming fully aware of what is going on within us and around us, and to do this without making a mess of it. And therein lies the rub.

How can we completely and deeply engage in life and its extraordinary display that we are a part of without making a mess of it? The key to this lies in our perceived need to interfere, to impinge upon it at one level or another, in order to make it feel personally meaningful to us. Our inability to allow it to be what it is marks the point at which impedance appears within the nerve system. That subtle flow of electromagnetism that keeps us alive becomes disrupted, and the expression of life becomes at some level subtly impaired.

When that interference in the experience comes to an end and life is utterly unimpaired, it flows frictionlessly through us. Without the interference of our mind, our nerve system should be effectively a superconductor; it simply flows the current of life through us.

But there it is, the predicament we are all faced with. We have this intelligence that has the capacity to recognise what we are a part of. Our recognition of this is what makes it all seem worthwhile and extraordinary. Yet that same intelligence has this inordinate capacity to think it knows best and impinge upon the experience, grasping or rejecting it or thinking it should be something other than it is, when in fact it is never anything other than what it is.

Of course, on hearing this there arises in our mind the objection, 'But does that mean we're supposed to live in some abject state of indolence and indifference?' No, it does not mean that. It means that what prompts you to act and engage in life should not be a rejection of, nor a grasping of, what is in front of you, but a complete willingness to accept it as it is.

I'm not suggesting that we do not completely jump right into the heart of life and fully engage with life. But thinking that it is mine and that it should be like this and should not be like that is the root justification for the myriad ways in which we interfere with it. This not only makes it messy but causes it to become dysfunctional.

It might be a very long time before the mind is subtle and concentrated enough to see behind the appearance of things to the process by which they arise. That need to understand is only our idea of ourself seeking justification, and as such we will always land upon the conclusions that suit us, or uphold our idea of ourselves, and reject the ones that undermine it.

Our journey out of suffering, to the point where our sense of separation from what we are experiencing ends, is the journey to that place where we are able to completely accept what is, as it is, and stop fighting with it. It may well take us on a rather roundabout route before we're able to let go and accept things as they are. We may need to seek some kind of personal resolution in order to feel able to let go, but what we are engaged in here is not a personal process. It is not personal. The universe does not behave differently for you than it does for anyone else.

Taking life personally is the root of all our misery. However unique an experience of it we personally may be having, the process of life itself is not personal. That intelligence, that deeper intelligence that is at work in all life, allowing it to express itself perfectly wherever it is allowed to, is not working one way on you and a different way on me and a different way elsewhere on something else.

It is a single process and it does not vary in the way in which it functions, however it may vary in the way it manifests or expresses itself. It only ever expresses itself as a pure expression of conditions. What we are experiencing is not personal, but it is a personal opportunity to witness the extraordinary thing, the miracle if you like, that life is.

It is our taking it personally that is our undoing. And the point at which we stop taking it personally is the point at which we can start to enter truly into life and allow life to move through us unimpeded. And it is only at that point that we might get to glimpse it, see it undistorted and come to know it for what it actually is.

So the first stage on the path of untangling this tangled knot, whether it is suffering or sickness or confusion or despair, the first stage to get to that place of peace, happiness and contentment, is the process of reorganising ourselves energetically enough so that some sense of coherence can be experienced within us individually.

In that way we can start to connect, find something that we feel we can lean upon, trust a little bit. Only as we come into coherence with what is around us does a sense that there might be an intelligence behind this life, that is underpinning it and holding it together, start to emerge. For as long as we remain in conflict with the way of things, seeking to bend it to our personal will, that higher intelligence remains cut off, choked and unable to express itself through us.

Up until that point, we have assumed that it is this personal will of ours that is the galvanising and driving force behind life. For as long as that is the case, we cannot begin to contemplate relinquishing our perceived need to feel in control, which is one of the greatest causes of interference with a process that we are not in control of. The more we insist on feeling, being or creating the sense or perception of being in control, the more we are going to atrophy that expression of life within us.

The only moment that you will be in control is when you utterly, utterly allow it to be what it is without rejecting it or seeking to grasp it. No matter how hard you try in every other moment, no matter how much control you exert over it, when you choose to relax you will not be able to relax completely, because you will not be in control, because you will always know that if you have bent your world to your will, the moment you relax it will start to fall apart.

Surrendering our control is a huge part of letting go. And in order to surrender we have to feel that we can trust it. The reason we feel we cannot trust the intelligence behind our lives is because it is so poorly expressed within us. It is so poorly expressed on account of the degree to which we are entangled and to which we interfere with it. Again it is a Catch-22: 'I won't let go until I know it will be OK to let go.' But you will not know that it is OK until you let go.

The gradual, step by step process of yielding our need to be in control and coming to a place of trust in this intelligence is a very personal journey. That sense that we can trust it comes upon us gradually. Reaching that place is what we call grace.

That is the point at which your sense of separation from what you are experiencing, and what you feel a part of, comes to an end. It is the point at which the sense of yourself that you put at the forefront of your experience fades in stages, revealing in its wake the simple suchness of what you have actually always been experiencing without realising it. It is to meet this point where our sense of separation ends, and to feel connected to that, this is the greatest longing that we have inside us.

And the only reason we have tangled ourselves up in knots and interfered with it so incessantly is because we have not learned to pay enough attention to it to see what is actually going on. The personal meaning that we seek in the end reveals itself to be only a kind of vanity, a need to be personally seen or met, and in the final analysis it reveals itself to be a compensation for not seeing the bigger picture. But life itself is inherently meaningful – turning up for it completely is the meaningful experience, not the story you tell yourself.

So when we start to sit and meditate, agitation, restlessness, frustration, discomfort, whatever it is that we experience that is not a state of serenity and peace or connectedness, this is the charge that we have accumulated throughout the life, that we are holding in the subtle electrical field at a software level and in our nerve system at a hardware level. This is our net stock of interference with that intelligence that I have just been explaining.

What we are actually talking about here is the feeling of not being able to be with ourselves. And that is actually our deepest suffering: not being able to be with this moment and the next and the next, which is all there ever is. That is what suffering really is.

And the cessation of suffering is being completely willing and able to be with it, to delight in being with it when the special things in life come our way, eventually to find a delight even in the ordinary in every moment. It is being able to be with it with a sense of wonder and joy, and when it is truly challenging, to accept that it is that way and find the kind of humility, patience and grace that means we can even be with that.

It is to work patiently towards that point – this is the invitation that meditation presents to us, this is the invitation that we accept when we sit on the cushion and decide to stay patiently and start to really pay attention. It is an invitation to learn to be with ourselves. It could not be more pure. There is nothing added externally that is going to make it an extraordinary event. It is just you, in the most ordinary moment of all, which one day will become the most extraordinary moment of all.

So when you find that you are not resting effortlessly within yourself and you cannot leave things alone to settle naturally, when you insist on playing with it, or messing about with it, or in the daily life when you find yourself interfering with others and not allowing them to be, just stop. Pay attention to how it feels. Any unwillingness to be with your experience, try to overcome it.

And in that way, that which does feel like friction will in stages pass, until there comes a point where there is not a sense of friction, where there is no conflict. And in that moment there will be no needing to be anywhere else but where you are right now. And that is the cessation of suffering.

There is no stone you have to look under so that one day you might find that mysterious key that unlocks the door to the solution to all your problems. It is not on the other side of the world in some exotic location, or at the foot of some great sage. It is in an ordinary moment in an ordinary place with ordinary you, just as it is. And when that simple moment is enough, more than enough, when you see that it is already complete, then the rest of life is a dance; an extraordinary opportunity to dance, fearlessly but lovingly and unobtrusively in this world.

I am not suggesting that it is easy. Real meditation is not easy. It is probably the hardest thing we will ever do, but it is so worth putting that much effort into, so that we can reach the point when we really can just be with ourselves, our lives and everything in it.

So that we can start to feel life within us, moving through us, around us. So that we can connect with it in a way that we did as children, when we trusted enough to be fully open to it. So that we can start to recognise what we have always been a part of. Something perhaps far more wonderful and extraordinary than all the things we have thus far tried to dream it up to be.

# CHAPTER FOUR

# THE LOSS OF CONSCIOUSNESS IN A LIFE WITHOUT SPIRITUAL CONTEXT

The human life without a spiritual context has a certain evolutionary process of its own. The course of a human life evolves according to a certain way which we can just watch happening. The coming into being, the birth, the growth, the development of our idea of ourself, the emergence of our sense of ourself within the world, our experience of living within the world, the gradual decay and breaking apart of that towards the end of life, and finally death.

And without the spiritual context, what we appear to have is the expression of matter becoming conscious for a period and then unconscious, and that is really what life appears to represent. The human life would evolve to the point where, as it comes out of infancy, it starts to relate to its position in relation to those around it as separate. It identifies itself as one thing, identifies others as another, creates ideas of itself in a position amongst what it is a part of and creates a highly individualised sense of itself.

So our personality is a reflection of our efforts to convey or project our individualised sense of who we think we are out to the world. And then without any connection to a higher aspect of consciousness, be that through religious devotion or spiritual enquiry and meditation, we evolve that idea of ourselves to the best of our ability, informed by parents, friends at school and peer groups, and our own ideas as we relate personally to the information and examples and influences and conditions that we meet. So we create this multi-layered sense of self that becomes highly individualised, and as far as we believe as humans at this time in history, highly evolved.

In the past few generations we have reached the pinnacle of individuality. If you look at the influences upon us now, everything is pointing towards trying to express ourselves as individually as possible. And everything is galvanised around the idea of me as the unit, what I can display to the world, and what kind of responses I can elicit. Social media today is a reflection of our obsession with this created idea of self and the need to feel that it is seen by others.

When we look at the way social media is organised and the way children now relate to themselves at school and what they aspire to, we often see that their aspirations are to be better than the person next to them or to become the person who is going to elicit the most admiration from others. One who feels unable to do that might be prone to suffer from a sense of worthlessness, despair or depression.

This is the way the planet evolves over a very, very long period of time. And at that level, the human being appears to be the most evolved expression of life because most life evolves only to the point of being sexually aware, with that sexual polarity being the galvanizing energy behind life.

Even as humans, the sexual energy and the desire to procreate is the strongest motivating energy in life. Even the desire to accumulate more possessions and status is largely governed by the fact that by being stronger or more elaborate in our display, we will attract the best mate.

When we try to deconstruct life by merely observing the ways in which it expresses itself materially, we tend to come to the belief that life is just a rare occurrence of matter becoming conscious under certain circumstances. It is all too easy to come to this view when we look out around us, because there is not much hinting at something beyond that. So it is understandable that we should come to the conclusions we do, and this is the basis of both materialist and nihilist views.

In a world such as this, here we are in our life working very hard to establish our position, vying for it, negotiating it, fighting for it, standing up for it, struggling to uphold it. We reach a stage, around about twenty-seven, twenty-eight, twenty-nine years old, when we become mature as an adult and that process of growth reaches a peak. The vital forces have already peaked and our mental capacities have likewise started to reach a peak. We may choose to sit down and train them but the process of growing up is complete, and the process of ageing and decay begins.

So we have created this idea of ourselves, and now there lies ahead of us the rest of our lives in which to express that idea of ourselves to the world, and off we go seeking friendships, partnerships, positions and so on, engaging in experiences that express and uphold this idea of me. And somewhere along the line it might dawn upon us, 'This expansive process that I've been utterly immersed in actually is now not expanding anymore.' And we might look forward and realise that there will be a time in the future when we are going to die.

Then we have an existential crisis as we look ahead and reflect upon the inevitability of that, but we still continue to try and hold this idea of ourself together, even in our hospital bed when we are told we only have a month to live, desperately trying to hold this idea of ourself together, trying to find a way out of the predicament we find ourselves in. The predicament we find ourselves in is the fact that everything we have invested our entire life in is about to be stripped away. And at that point, quite often, people start to pray or start to ask for spiritual guidance or open up in some way.

That is the way that life runs its course, and with it comes the gradual passing away. The gradual onset of old age brings a letting go because we cannot move physically as much as we used to, we cannot do as much as we used to, we cannot gather as much energy around us as we used to, we cannot project ourselves out into the world with as much force and dynamism as we used to. So there is a process of having to relinquish that creates something of a spiritual reflection on our apparent demise. We realise that this life is inevitably going to come to an end.

But what is going to come to an end? My idea of myself will come to an end; this personal and individual expression of life that I have spent my whole life orchestrating and developing is going to come to an end.

And so, without any spiritual context to our life at all, never having reflected upon whether there might be anything beyond this, or having ignored or denied or refused to accept the possibility that there might be, we face our end.

The way the mind meets its death is like this. The consciousness withdraws from the sense doors, the same way it does when we go to sleep. It drops into unconsciousness and comes to rest in the heart, the same way as it does at night. And in the same way as we do when we dream, the unconscious impressions in what we shall for now just call our unconsciousness, or our memory, or what the Buddha called bhavaṅga[1], begin to surface and our unconscious plays itself out.

Now your conscious mind, lacking any spiritual context, will have become organised around your idea of yourself, and death brings the sudden realisation that that is now being stripped away. So what happens as we die is that our attention fixates upon the strongest impressions we are holding in our conscious or unconscious memory and desperately tries to grasp and hold onto the things we are most attached to. Of all the impressions we have accumulated in our memory throughout the life, there are two types that pull us most strongly in the dying process: it tends either to be a single experience that has left a very strong reaction or weighty impression in our memory, or a habitual reaction that has gone on in the mind many, many times. Those single impressions that have left an extremely strong impact pull upon us as we go through the dying process. These impressions will be either of attachment and grasping, or aversion and rejecting, or in the case of positive mental states very strong impressions of love, appreciative joy and gratitude. Eventually the mind will latch onto the one single impression which has left the strongest impact and around which we carry the strongest charge. We then pass away with this impression in our consciousness. It is the quality and

---

1 For a full explanation of this process please see 'The Flavour of Liberation', Vol. 1, Chapter 31, and Vol. 3, Chapter 31.

nature of that impression, be it wholesome or unwholesome, that we latch onto during this dying process that determines what happens next.

Now, at this point I understand I am explaining a process that is not in any way obvious to our ordinary field of perception. We cannot observe with the naked eye what happens to consciousness after the moment of death. All we can do is observe that it no longer continues to appear within the body. If we have reached the conclusion that consciousness was produced by the body as a sign of life, then now that the body is not living any more, we assume that consciousness itself must have ceased without remainder.

One of the first things we learn to investigate, once we have developed concentration capable of breaking down the apparent compactness of our experience, is the nature of material and mental processes and their causes. If we are in any way going to break free of the materialist paradigm and come to understand what the Buddha was trying to show us— or what many of the other spiritual traditions throughout history have tried to show us, which is that consciousness does not come to cessation with the stopping of the heart—then we will need to develop the capacity to break down this appearance of compactness to witness the causal process or creative principles at work behind it.

What comes to cessation at death is the subtle material support for the arising of consciousness within the body. This is what I have called the software system. The hardware (the body) is no longer capable of running the software package (consciousness), and so consciousness stops appearing within the body.

One of the milestones in spiritual insight comes through our meditation practice when we witness for ourselves that it is not the body (or matter) that is producing consciousness but consciousness that is producing matter. We witness this happening. There is no way I can convince anyone of this in a book, and it is not my intention to do so. It is one of the processes that the Buddha himself acknowledged was deep and both hard to perceive and hard to grasp.

Normally we pass on at the end of the life with the quality of the mind that we have effectively been most fixated upon, which is our idea of ourself that we have spent our life creating. And of course it is only at that point that one who has never deeply investigated this process will come to know what actually happens.

So this is the human life without a spiritual context and it might be very convenient to come to the conclusion that, 'Yes, none of my actions have any real consequences because I'm here for just a brief time, and when I'm gone, I'm gone.' It is the perfect invitation to selfishness and so we indulge ourselves in the pursuit of everything we personally want, hoping that it is just curtains and nothing more when we die. And if that was the case then it would be fine to spend this life entirely invested in ourselves and in the expression of ourselves to the world and then to give it all up with our final breath.

But even if that were the case, we have to ask ourselves, 'What would the world look like inhabited largely by beings who took that position?' Well, basically, we would have a world pretty much as we see it now.

In spite of the fact that we can observe clearly the effects of our actions upon others and the world around us at a macro level, in spite of the fact that we know categorically that we have been taking out more than we put in, at alarming rates, the pull of the pursuit of our desires and the continued projection of ourselves out to the world prompts us to pretend to ourselves at both an individual and group level that we have not seen what we have seen, in order to justify our continued pursuits.

It is not that we lack intelligence. We are intelligent. But the Buddha did not claim that suffering was caused by stupidity, but by ignorance. Ignorance is not paying attention to how things are. That is the real cause of suffering.

The point is that consciousness does not just tend towards the selfish projection of ourselves upon the world. There are deeper human feelings that arise within us such as love, compassion and empathy that are anything but selfish responses to the world, and they are all prompted by a deep feeling of connectedness to something that is beyond this idea of myself.

The Buddha used to talk of two kinds of beings, those who are view-rooted: who relate their experience to their ideas of the world and themselves within it, and those who are experience-rooted: who relate to their experience through how it feels directly.

When one who is view-rooted looks out upon a material universe and witnesses things like love and compassion, they might come to the view that they are the response of beings trying to make sense of their life, or add meaning to their personal perspective.

Likewise they would argue that our ideas of a creative intelligence behind life, are ideas we create in our mind which serve the purpose of trying to make life feel meaningful, when it is not inherently so.

But the truth is that love is not simply an idea that arises in our mind. It is a deeply felt, embodied experience and it arises almost universally as a response to being open to life in a way that transcends the mind and its ideas.

Those of us who are experience-rooted feel what is happening within us and what is happening to those around us, recognising that we are all sharing a common experience: the experience of being alive. We likewise start to recognise that we are connected at a deeper level than we may appear to be. Our capacity to feel deeply for each other is in no way a cerebral process, but a deeply embodied, felt experience.

When we start to pay enough attention at an experiential level to what is going on within us and around us, rather than trying to figure it all out at the level of ideas, we witness the gradual dismantling of our isolated sense of self, and the gradual emergence or recognition of a deeper intelligence behind our lives, through which we are all connected to each other.

This inner conviction does not come upon us because we join up the dots or put all the pieces of the jigsaw together, it comes through at a much deeper level than that of our concrete ideas. In fact, we may spend most of our lives not fully understanding how or why we feel the way we do, but simply knowing that we do.

Now how does this relate to what happens if we add a spiritual context into our lives? Whatever that spiritual context might be, whether it starts with meditation or prayer or just a deeper reflection upon life, what is it that prompts us to start opening up at a heart level?

The opening of the heart starts not with the certainty that we understand anything, but with the acceptance that it is OK that we do not know. And this, in turn, matures into a state of surrender and grace.

It is probably the case that we start meditating from some kind of self-focused perspective, 'What's my life all about? Who am I? How can I find peace?' We sit down and we start to investigate it with the question of 'Who am I?' right at the forefront of our minds. But it is through the very investigation that meditation brings about, that the 'Who am I?' starts to be dismantled, as we open up to the understanding that it is not about me, that there is something bigger at work here.

Through a devotional attitude we might open our heart to an idea of some principle, and let's only call it a principle at this stage, some governing principle that is out there to be discovered that we do not understand. Maybe we call it God, and it may well be an idea that we inherited through views that have been passed down to us. Although we do not really know anything about whether they are true or not, there is something that is instilled in us that prompts us to look beyond the obvious for a deeper truth behind our lives.

Where we look does not actually matter when we start, because it is the looking for a deeper meaning itself that opens the heart to the idea that it is not all about me and that there is something beyond the appearance of things. We cannot understand why we feel love, but we certainly know that we do. Real love is the longing for the happiness of another. Why would we feel this, if it was all about me? The point is, we would not.

As intelligent beings, we may even go on to formulate some kind of spiritual context at an intellectual level. That is when we use our own individual consciousness to try to create context to our lives and we look out upon the world seeking answers at the level of ideas. We then rally behind this view without ever knowing if it is right or not.

The best we can do is to look out upon the world as it appears to be and hypothesise around these appearances. From such a perspective we might come to the idea that God and this idea of connectedness are created in the mind simply to add a sense of meaning to our lives. This is the end point for the view-rooted perspective, as mentioned earlier. From the view-rooted perspective we might consider God and connectedness and then decide whether to reject or accept it as an idea, but without having worked towards an experience of such things.

On the opposite side of the fence, when we pray, we invite into our lives something that we have the humility to accept may be beyond our current understanding, and acknowledge we do not yet know. In Christianity we have the idea of a creator being, in Buddhism the idea of an intelligent creative process. But both of them hold onto the belief that the creative process itself is perfect.

Whether it is Jesus or a saint of the past, whether it is Buddha, or whether we are simply moved by the experience we have, be it of love or suffering, to the point of entering more completely into it at a level that is beyond our concrete understanding, does not matter. But when we do first start to encounter it, a part of us begins to look beyond ourselves for inspiration and meaning in our lives. And that is the point at which the heart opens, and the mind that insists on knowing has to acknowledge that it does not.

Once we start to open up to it, we gradually come to  recognise that there *is* an intelligence at work which holds our life together, which flourishes when our mind is out of the way, when we are asleep or in deep meditation. But it atrophies and becomes impeded when our conditioned mind ,and our ideas of self, hold sway. It is there every night when we fall asleep even though we do not recognise it. In those moments when we are out of the way, it reorganises and refreshes us. And it does so in ways that we do not fully understand but that we know we totally rely upon.

While we are in a deep sleep, we come to rest in a state of consciousness that we are not aware of, which contains this profound capacity to maintain our lives. Far from the kind of active intelligence that arises within our mind when we are ordinarily awake, it is, in fact, a state of pure, luminous awareness and clarity, and we can often live our entire lives ignorant of its presence or existence.

Jesus acknowledged that it was something that eluded concrete understanding, calling it the 'peace that passeth all understanding'. If we can practise meditation and maintain awareness when our mind comes to cessation, we will start to enter deeply into this state. If then we are able to maintain awareness as we fall asleep, we will also witness for ourselves this same state of pure luminosity as the place that we rest in while appearing to be dead to the world.

And we will witness its extraordinary capacity to repair and reorganise all the incoherence that the mind has produced, with all its lofty ideas of itself. If we can come to recognise it, it is this same state of luminosity that will reveal itself to us when we die.

And this is what Jesus and the Buddha were trying to point us towards in their different ways. What is more, they both suggested that it is our failing to recognise it, both within our lives and in the moment of our death, that brings us to so much unnecessary suffering. It is the 'not knowing' of this that the Buddha states is the fundamental ignorance that is the ultimate cause of suffering.

This intelligence is always and everywhere sitting in the background, doing what it can to keep life in balance, within us and around us. It has kept all life perfectly in balance for millions of years before the emergence of humanity and its personal will. When we live in alignment with that intelligence we flourish, when we live in conflict with it we flounder.

Even when we fall into sheer delusion, and our life becomes nothing but an expression of our personal will, that intelligence does not stop functioning. It simply becomes so interfered with that there is little sign left of its functioning.

We are close to such a situation in the world today, where humanity's will is expressed to the extreme, but the creative intelligence behind our lives has almost been cut off. We can keep ourselves alive artificially now, but while the human intelligence and its ability to impose its will is developing, our connection to this higher consciousness itself may well be degenerating in ways that we are not recognising.

So what role does meditation play in reconnecting us to this higher intelligence? When we come to meditation for the first time, we often do so seeking to support our life at a personal level. We start to work out some of our personal challenges and we start to refine our character and reorganise our ego, by knocking off the rough edges, developing more patience, more feeling of compassion, less feeling of judgement, less feeling of arrogance, more feeling of humility. And hopefully a little more peace in our lives.

All of these things are wonderful, and that refining of the character is very important in bringing us to the point where we are willing to surmount our idea of ourselves in favour of a higher principle by allowing the heart to open.

This opening of the heart allows us to start to feel what is happening to us at a deeper level. Our capacity to feel is the result of awareness moving fluidly through us. When awareness stagnates around fixed ideas and attitudes, our capacity to feel likewise stagnates. If this happens too much then we are left with only our ideas to fill the gap in our experience.

If this goes on for too long we end up inhabiting a virtual inner world that is entirely subjective, with very little connection to the actual world we are a part of. We have reached a point today in life where, because our ability to connect to what we feel has been so shut down on a number of fronts, our virtual world feels more compelling to us than our actual world. This marks the point of the degeneration of consciousness where we lose our connection to the creative process, as we become totally intoxicated with the idea of ourselves as the creator.

This loss of feeling at a fundamental level is another form of ignorance that leads to suffering. Although we may not be physically afflicted or experiencing obvious hardships, the numbness that comes upon us as we lose our capacity to feel starts to disconnect us from our sense of deeper meaning to our lives. And in its absence we turn instead to the pursuit of our desires in our efforts to find happiness and fulfilment.

However, as we open up through the practice of meditation, and start to let go some of these fixed ideas and the charge around them, there comes a point where we start to reconnect to our feelings again and their ability to show us where we might be in conflict. We stop being informed only by the ideas that we are able to formulate, and start to relate to the actual experience we are having.

Gradually there comes a point at which, instead of working at a level of ideas and principles that we seek to uphold, or trying to join up the dots, we acknowledge that this pursuit of a personal resolution is not ultimately getting us anywhere. This is when we start to connect again to that higher intelligence and start to recognise how it is expressing itself through life at a deeper level.

Now how does that start to work on us energetically? We start to recognise that aspect of consciousness which we connect to through the heart and which is beyond our concrete ideas. We start to align more with this state of pure awareness in the background of our lives. In our meditation, we begin to recognise that basic state of pure awareness, within which our mind, with all its elaborate ideas, merely arises and passes, moment to moment. We turn our focus from the display to the process by which it is arising, and gradually this starts to become our reference point.

We see the ideas and thought-forms, and associations and reactions and feelings and perceptions that arise within the mind to colour our experience as something that is secondary to the actual experience itself. The experience itself is arising within that ground of pure awareness. And we start to recognise that the pull and distraction and intoxication with the things we seek to add to our experience with our mind, are actually merely robbing us of the experience itself.

Gradually we start to stand upon the basic ground of awareness, and we start to surrender the personal will and all its ideas, allowing this higher intelligence to become our teacher.

We start to gradually, in stages, look into and see that what appeared at first to be a process of matter becoming consciousness, actually is the process of consciousness becoming matter. We see that it is not the idea of myself that is sitting in the background, but that there is a fundamental primal ground to existence that is the basis for the arising of everything of which we are a part. Now we start to establish a more universal context for our existence rather than an individual one.

Then we start to look to the future and the time that we will die and ask, 'What is it that is dying?' And we may not know the answer yet, but our questions are starting to turn themselves around. We gradually start to recognise that apart from our instinctive, creative urge that drives most of our desires, there is a higher creative principle at work that is bringing things into being out of this basic all-pervasive ground of awareness. We recognise that there is a higher longing within us which is the longing to experience and come to know directly what it is that connects us to all things.

# PART II

───── ◆ ─────

## THE SECOND NOBLE TRUTH: THE CAUSE OF SUFFERING

─────────────

## BEYOND APPEARANCES — WHY ARE WE SUFFERING?

# CHAPTER FIVE

# OUR RITE OF PASSAGE

**W**hat is the essence of what the Buddha was trying to teach us? It is easy to get lost in ideas with all these teachings of the Buddha, the Eightfold Noble Path, the Four Noble Truths, the Dharma, Dependent Origination and so on. But really everything he taught was pointing at one thing and one thing alone. One day he picked up a handful of leaves from the forest floor and turned to his assistant Ananda and said, 'You know, Ananda, these leaves in my hand represent the knowledge I have shared with you, which is for the cessation of suffering. All the leaves on the forest floor represent all the knowledge that there is.' He did not teach what he taught to satisfy folk's thirst for knowledge. He taught out of compassion, desiring others to be free from suffering.

He had only a single wish, and that was to show the way out of suffering, having realised it for himself. He wanted to show what suffering is, what are its causes and the way out of it. He never spoke unprompted and when he did speak he was very direct. He did not pander to people's sensitivities but spoke a truth that related directly to their predicament. He was pretty brutal on that account because what actually constitutes the cessation of suffering is something that takes tremendous maturity to accept.

It may well be that it takes us a while before each of us feels ready to imbibe the essence of what the Buddha was telling us. When I say it takes maturity I do not mean that in a judgemental way, but rather in relation to our evolution. This occurs as we go through processes in the life and from one lifetime to another. Certain stages in our process of evolving, as we pass through them, will create in us fundamental changes in our attitude towards life.

I often speak about the path out of suffering as a rite of passage. The rite of passage that the Eightfold Noble Path represents is the rite of passage out of spiritual adolescence into spiritual maturity. I do not mean the idea that when you reach twenty-two years old you should be a fully mature woman or man. I am talking about the transformation of our conscious perspective upon life which prompts us to function in a completely different way, with full spiritual maturity, as opposed to the self-focused, egoic attitude of adolescence.

In the process of growing up there are phases in our life when it is most definitely all about me. When you are born you are just a pure expression of life - although anyone who has had children knows that children do not arrive as completely blank pages. We do bring something with us, but it is a relatively clean start. Whatever we bring into life, it is still a fresh start. And then we grow up and as we do so we gradually develop this extraordinarily complex idea of ourselves. There comes a point when our whole universe is all about me; we are absolutely at the centre of the universe and we are the most important thing in it and if we are not attended to, then our world is going to fall apart.

Now this egoic sense of self is very strong in some and not so strong in others. Maybe you have had children, maybe you have had more than one child and I am sure you can see that some children come through and they have an enormous sense of their own personal needs or an enormous need to be seen. And there are other children who come through who are quite happy to chip along and do their thing without the need to be seen.

This need to be seen evolves and gets more elaborate as we transition from childhood into adolescence, at which point life is very much about staking our claim on the world and making sure that the world knows who I am.

Then there comes a point when we ought to make the transition into adulthood, from being an extremely will-driven, volitional person who is at the centre of our universe, into a more selfless, mature person willing to be a functional member of the group. And this is our rite of passage. It's the point at which we leave our adolescent perspective behind and ascend into full adulthood, willing to serve and perform our function and play our part in maintaining the functionality of the group as a whole.

The Buddha talked about humans as being volitional (will-driven) or functional (responsive to the needs of the group). The unawakened being he called volitional is someone driven by personal will and the desire to make the world the way they want it, to move things in the direction that they perceive they should go. An awakened being is what he called a functional being, performing their function seamlessly so they are a contributor and not an inconvenience to others around them in the way in which they live. They do not draw upon others or create a mess in the way that they do things.

So when we actually get to that point of being functional, it does not actually matter what the function is, because we are seated right within the root of ourselves as a being, knowing that performing that function is part of what allows the universe to continue to turn without conflict. And that transition out of adolescence into adulthood is the point at which we let go the idea of who I think I want to become, should be, am meant to be, and find out who we actually are. By only pursuing our egoic ambitions regardless of how appropriate they are, we often create chaos, confusion and conflict.

Of course, when we are adolescent there are all sorts of ideas of who we would like to grow up to be that run amok in our head and it is all about being the most important person. What is the single biggest marker of adolescence? The idea that I am special. What is the first thing we are going to need to get over if we are going to make that transition into adulthood? It is getting over the idea that we are special. It is realising we are not special. There are eight billion of us here and not long after we are gone no one is going to know we were here. Someone who thinks they are special makes a right old hoo-ha going about doing what they are doing and is often a nuisance to those around them.

A special human being is one who is able to move seamlessly in this world without creating a stink, but who contributes positively to the welfare of others while doing so. Such a person lives without being an inconvenience to others, without drawing or pulling energy from others, without poaching energy off others in order to be seen or to get their way, without imposing their energy all over others in the process of being here. Such a person may go totally unnoticed in the world, but what they contribute is greater than what they take.

Now if we can accept this invitation to grow up gracefully, then we will discover that our needs are far fewer than we thought and we are far more likely to make a positive contribution with our lives. If we cannot grow up and accept it gracefully, we take our adolescent attitude into what ought to be adulthood. In doing so we create inconvenience all around us, for ourselves and others, and generally become hard to serve and of many needs. In this way it is easy to become someone who takes far more than they give back in life.

Now, this is what it is to come into mature adulthood and it does not mark you as more special than the next person. It ought to mark you as the same, because it points to the fact that you have recognised the unity and connectedness between you and the next person, rather than that sense of separation. In a functional society that ought to happen naturally in the process of growing up and indeed sometimes it does, and sometimes it does not. We may still be stuck in a very childish attitude towards ourselves and others even when we are fifty or sixty. We may even die with this attitude. So this rite of passage into full adulthood or full maturity does not necessarily happen in the life. It may, or it may not.

One of my students provides support to those who are in positions of great authority, at the top of big companies and institutions. He has said to me on a number of occasions that he meets many people whose lives are totally held together by those below them because they cannot function effectively in the position of great responsibility in which they have found themselves.

Now there are people out there who are struggling. There are people out there who are merely coping. And there are people out there who are flourishing. What they do with their lives has no bearing upon whether they are struggling, coping or flourishing. I can tell you that some of the most confused, dysfunctional human beings on the planet are the people in positions of power and leadership, because they got there as an act of personal will, driven by ambition rather than simply as a reflection of their merits.

When such a person reaches a position of authority they often have no idea how to hold the energy that they are supposed to hold. This causes no end of inconvenience to everybody beneath them who are running around like headless chickens, trying to keep the show on the road. It creates a mess. One well-organised assistant or one well-organised administrator is infinitely more important, even if they do not recognise it, than a messy leader.

A poorly-organised leader makes a far greater mess than most. A well-organised assistant, for example, makes the world around them function beautifully. A teacher who is a mess creates chaos and confusion. An administrator who is shambolic, who is in the position of keeping the show on the road but is actually poorly organised, creates a mess. But a well-organised administrator keeps the cogs turning and is far more important than the leader.

The point is that if, in our narcissism, we strive for more influence and power than is appropriate, it is not only the cause of our own suffering, but of great suffering for others. This is why I always say we should reflect deeply upon the difference between our ambition, our drive to be the best, and our aspiration, our desire to do our best.

The idea that the most important person is the person at the top is a figment of our own imagination, rooted in the idea that we need to be special and have to be seen as important to feel special.

Society seems to be hung up on the idea that 'I need to be special, more special than the next person, or at least more important'. It is not necessary, it is nonsense. There are lots and lots of very wilful people out there making a nuisance and making a mess, making life incredibly difficult for others, in various ways.

It is not about who we think we want to be, 'I want to be a leader, I want to be a rock star.' These are figments of our own imagination dreamed up by our ego. Even the idea that 'I want to be an activist who is going to change the world,' if rooted in a deep feeling of anger and resentment at the way things are, is going to cause more conflict than it resolves.

Behind all our elaborate egoic ideas of what we think we need to be, there is a function which, when you start performing it, you unfold at a soul level and flourish. In fact, very often it is only when we start doing things that we might have thought would be completely contrary to our initial ideas, do we start to develop and grow beyond the place that we are currently at.

So it is important to let go the idea of 'How important can I be?' or, 'How special can I be?' and start to reflect upon 'How useful, helpful and functional can I be?'

To do this we need to get in touch with our own soul, and take the focus off our idea of ourselves and who we think we need to be and what we think we have got to show the world. The world is not interested. Because sooner or later we will be gone, and then not long after that we will be forgotten. The real thing is whether we were able to turn up completely in our life and recognise what we are a part of.

A skilful human being moves like a stick through water and does not leave that much of a trace. A skilful human being is not an inconvenience to the world that they are a part of, but contributes in some way that goes unnoticed. That is what it is to be functional. So when you set your stall out and decide where you think you need to go in this life, there is only one thing that makes your life a real act of merit, and that is service. There are countless ways of serving, of being a contributor. It does not mean you have to be special. Going unnoticed means you can get on with the job of doing and being, performing your function.

One of the greatest acts of service and merit is the selfless love of raising children. In fact, parenting is the pathway by which most people renew their merit in this life, through serving selflessly those in their care. But of course, it is equally the area in which we can, through selfishness, fail to renew our merit.

And yet today, we see governments pressured into supporting parents to get back to work as soon as possible after a child is born, because the household is so expensive to maintain that both parents have to work. Both the mother and father are often having to work so that they can afford to pay for childcare. This is quite possibly the single biggest indicator of how our modern society has become lost and fixated upon status and material gain, and lost sight of the real value of service and contribution. I cannot imagine there being many people who have positions at work where they are needed more than they are needed by their children.

The point at which we choose to become parents is the point at which we are put through our rite of passage, if we have not already gone through it. If we do not transition out of our adolescent fixation with ourselves and learn at that point how to serve selflessly, then we can easily start to bring suffering not just to ourselves but to others. It seems that rather than seeing the raising of children as the highest of honours, the stay-home parent is now almost marginalised.

Sometimes parents seem willing to pass the opportunity to serve their children on to others so that they can continue their pursuit of prestige, material gain and status. We need to reflect seriously on this, because it is much harder to make merit with our lives elsewhere than it is through the raising of a functional and supported family unit.

So, deportment that is bent on personal gain and conduct that seeks the approval of some, often at the expense of others, is vanity. It is rooted in pride and our need to compare ourselves to others as better. We also need to get over the idea that we might think we are not as good. It is a nonsense. A functional human being does not compare themselves to others. They just get on with the job of being who they are.

And when you are performing your function coherently, extraordinary things can be done with the slightest of gestures that might take very little energy to do, but they can make a profound difference. Because it is not an act of imposing your will upon the world to make things happen, it is just an alignment with a current that is working through you.

As human beings, or groups of people, we do not have a very good track record of getting on well for long periods of time. Sooner or later people bang their heads together with their egos or ideas of self. It is not until a group self-organises at a functional level that the individuals comprising it stop comparing themselves to others and vying for position, worrying how important they are, and just put their heads down and get on. And that is when a group functions, a collective functions, flourishes and evolves.

When you are happy to be who you are, performing whatever function it is, and delighting in the doing of it, you play your part in the growth of everybody around you. But when you are messy or ego-driven, performing a function without having deeply within you the skills to do it, that is a mismatch between who you are and the energy that you have got, and what you are trying to achieve. In this way, the group does not flourish.

So in the dialogue we are all having now about evolving to a higher level of consciousness, we need to ask ourselves, 'Are we really waking up?' When reflecting on the evolution into mature adulthood at a group level, we need to understand that we are living in an adolescent society. We are not living in one that is driven by mature adult principles. We are living in a society that is driven by the perceived need to compare ourselves to others as better, same or worse. Our value as a human being is written in terms of how I compare to the next person in terms of the display I can show the world.

That is not how you will be judged when you finally pass. You will not be judged. All you will take with you is the quality of your mind and the merit or lack of it that you have made with your life. You will either be at peace with yourself or you will not, and that is the mind you will take on with you.

So let us get over all this lunacy of trying to prove something. It is a nonsense. We are here to find peace with what it is that we are a part of, and when we have found it, we will find our own way to function beautifully. So make your priority making peace with yourself and trust that you will find your position in this world along the way. And be prepared to be surprised by where you end up. And be open to it.

In our approach to life, how does this transition into adulthood actually express itself? Sloth and torpor is one of the major hindrances in life, and this is our unwillingness to do what needs to be done. It is, in effect, laziness. Other hindrances such as desire and greed are the perceived need to have something now, which stops us finding peace with what we have.

When we transition from adolescence into adulthood, our sloth and torpor need to be transformed into a willingness to do. Because, as our greed and desire become surmounted, it is our willingness to do that brings forth a new kind of enthusiasm and energy behind our lives.

This word willingness is a really key word – there is a big difference between wilfulness and willingness. It is our willingness that allows us to be with things as they are, and evolve with them and see every challenge as a teacher. It is our willingness to do what needs to be done that turns us into a functional contributor to the well-being of others.

It is important that we do not try to force this transition into adulthood upon ourselves too early in life, but it is also important that we embrace it when it is time. That does not mean that we do not carry with us a joyful, almost childlike, delight in life and what goes on around us. No-one is suggesting that in the process of growing up we should become dry. There is always room for something of the childlike wonder, that delight, that excitement, that adventure in life. But the broken adolescent principles that might have driven us, will someday have to be let go if we are going to make peace with ourselves.

But you do not have to make it happen now. It is not about trying to slay your ego. Recognise the role that time has to play, and get a sense of perspective on the journey that you are on. And then make friends with where you are at on that journey, and get a sense of where you are going.

If you are not yet ready to let go the ego, you may still feel the need to seek personal resolution to some of the wounds you carry. There is nothing wrong with this and there is no fixed rule about what time in our lives we become truly ready to let go. There is something in this life that has so much intelligence to it that a conscious human being who is open and trusting, though they may take knocks, will get to a place of grace by the end of it. So we take it on the chin. We get up, we get over it. And we slowly and in stages stop being a nuisance to ourselves and others.

This process might start on hearing something like this, or we might think 'What?!' But if we really get in touch with our heart and we are willing to listen to it, it is also the biggest relief to hear it. Because within that becoming functional will be your unique expression of what it is to be human. And that is deeply personal, and something to deeply connect with. And it is not dry, it is exquisitely alive. It just does not need to make a big splash or get a round of applause.

I tell the story of the yogi who comes up to his master and says, 'So, Master, what was it that you did before you were enlightened?' And he replies, 'Why, I chopped wood and carried water.' 'And now you're enlightened, what do you do?' 'Why, I chop wood and carry water.' It does not matter what you do if you can find a way of doing it with heart.

So give yourself permission to find out who you are, to meet yourself there, and just be what you came here to be. And do not worry about the fact that one day you will be gone and totally forgotten. Dance it while you are here, without making a nuisance of yourself. And see if you can get to that point where you can recognise and can touch the intelligence that rests in the background, that is taking care of you, that has never judged you, that is just waiting for you to make contact.

It is our awakening out of the friction of adolescence into mature adulthood, where ideas of self are not the reference point of our experience any more, that is the essence of the Buddha's Dharma. And it is easy to get lost with this, trying to fathom out what it is the Buddha is trying to say. We might think that he is telling us that there is no self there, there is no 'me', that this idea of me is an elaboration, a figment of our imagination, but we do not experience existence in that way. We experience very much a sense of ourselves as the galvanising force and influence within our lives. And yet we hear that this experience of no-self is our awakening.

The Buddha is teaching us about no-self, which is the hub, the pith, the core of this teaching. Dependent Origination, the whole chain of Dependent Origination, starts with ignorance. At the beginning of the causal chain of Dependent Origination is ignorance, which is not understanding that this idea of 'me' is a figment of my imagination, is an illusion, caused by my unwise attention to the experience I am involved in.

No-self is not an idea to grapple with. You cannot just sit there and say, 'Yes, the third Noble Truth is the realisation of no-self as the cessation of suffering' because most of the time we are jolly well experiencing ourself as ourself and we are right at the forefront of that experience. In which case no-self most certainly is not apparent to us, is it?

We are not talking about subscribing to that view. We are talking about the way in which we engage in the experience of life which brings an immediacy to it, that is not crowded out by a sense of self.

Gradually, as this egoic aspect of our mind gets relinquished, there is more and more immersion in what we are experiencing and less and less sense of me. This complete fixation on myself, my needs, my perception, how I relate to others, who I think others are, what I think my life is about, is nothing but a noise and a distraction that filters out the immediacy of our experience.

We are not talking about subscribing to the view or the idea of no-self. We are talking about an experience of no self. And it does not come from figuring it all out but by developing awareness to the point at which perception of self fades from our experience and we begin to enter more completely into it. That is not something that we can think through, although we can contemplate it to a degree. It either happens to us or it does not happen to us.

The process of making this transition, this rite of passage out of adolescence to the point at which we stand in a fully mature state, simply willing to participate in the experience of being alive, reaching the point of understanding that my idea of myself does not matter, takes a maturity that comes upon us gradually. You cannot make it happen. Some people's idea of self is extremely strong, is extremely elaborate, is extremely invested in, and this is why it often takes the experience of suffering to prompt them to relinquish it. In a way, we are often willing to suffer no end of affliction to hold on to this idea of ourself when actually that suffering would be so much less if we gave it up.

So how willing or unwilling are we to let go these ideas of ourself and meet who we actually are, as we are? How ready are we to move unnoticed in this world, knowing that it is enough just to be a part of it? Because that is the point of spiritual maturity or adulthood, when we are willing to relinquish and let go and free ourselves of all the energy that we have gathered around us for the purposes of showing the world who we are. That is what is exhausting, that is what takes endless upholding, that is how we haemorrhage most of our vitality when we are very fixated on self.

The less fixated on self we are, the less energy we have to spin around the upholding of it, the freer we are, the more spacious we become, the less we worry about the outcome, the less important the outcome is and the more we can move through life frictionlessly.

So have a look at it. Ask yourself, 'Am I ready to start unpacking the ego and leaving it behind?' No one is forcing you to do anything, and letting go is not something anyone can tell you that you must do. There is a timely unfolding at a soul level that happens when we are ripe for it. Often it takes suffering that we are not willing to forebear anymore, which prompts us to relinquish.

How far you have to suffer on account of your ego is actually entirely up to you. That is what pride is. This dogged insistence to keep 'me' in the equation and this insistence on comparing myself to others. 'Am I doing all right? Am I good enough? Am I as good? Am I better?' Whether it is arrogance or whether it is some sense of lack of self-esteem, it is all pride. Whether it is strong in you or weak in you is all dependent on how strongly you are attached to your idea of yourself.

Life is constantly inviting us to let go this idea of ourselves so that we can completely live it. If you see that and something clicks and your ideas start to be dismantled, there is a blissful and painless experience of letting go. If you are trying to let go your suffering, prompted only by your desire not to suffer, but there is an unwillingness to let go this idea of self or ego, then it is a painful letting go. This is part of what the Buddha meant when he said there are some who progress painlessly and others who progress painfully.

Life is complete without each of us and if any of us were to disappear in a puff of smoke right now, it would not skip a beat. When we can delight in that idea, instead of being horrified by it, we learn to really dance with life and to do whatever we do without clinging to it. It does not matter. The universe is not waiting for you to figure it out or waiting to hear what you have to say about it. It is waiting for you to turn up and experience it completely.

There is the rite of passage that the Eightfold Noble Path is pointing towards, and it is that transition out of adolescence into adulthood. It is the release of that huge amount of energy we spin around us and the interference which that produces in the universe, to that point of willingness to function as a functional member of the group.

You may well cut wood, carry water, chop vegetables, build a spaceship, discover the cure for cancer. It does not matter. You do it functionally, willingly, coherently, as part of your immersion in the process of life. But it does not matter. Engage completely, but understand it does not matter. Be sincere about what you do, but do not take yourself too seriously. That is what it is to be functional rather than volitional, having a willingness to do, rather than a desire and need to do.

Once our personal needs are few and we are both easy to serve and serve easily, we will not need to spin so much energy out of the universe in our direction. And once we reach that willingness to do, we will probably find ourselves making our own small contribution to the well-being of those around us.

# CHAPTER SIX

# A LOOK AT KARMA AND ITS WORKING

Let us start to look now at karma, at the law of karma, to try to see into how it actually might be functioning in our lives. By seeing into it, we can get beyond doubt about what karma is and get beyond the idea that karma is a view that we either subscribe to or do not. In this way, we can begin to feel it as a dynamic and active force at work in our lives at all times.

There is much confusion about the law of karma. Some people simply reject the whole idea that our past actions have a capacity to condition what happens to us in the present, and likewise that our present actions have a future effect. Because it is hard to see how the energy of karma is functioning within our lives, it is of course easy to reduce the notion of karma from being one of the strongest conditioning factors within our lives to something akin to a superstitious belief.

In the same way that some refute the whole notion of karma as one of the universal principles governing life, others lean too much in the other direction, subscribing to the view that everything in life is an expression of karma. This is also clearly not the case.

When the Buddha was asked about the natural order of the universe and the role that karma plays, he identified the law, or way, of karma as one of five significant conditioning factors within the overall 'way of things'. If we are going to reach a clear understanding and perspective on how and why the world and everything in it expresses itself the way it does, we need to understand karma within this wider context.

So the five governing principles which together account for the dynamic display of material and conscious phenomena that we observe in life are as follows:

1. **The Law of the Elements.** This is the natural order of non-living matter. At a micro level, it is the dynamic relationship between the four elements of earth, water, fire and air,[2] which expresses itself as the climatic conditions: the behaviour of fire, gases, water, soil, rocks and minerals. Most natural disasters such as floods and earthquakes would be governed by this.

Put into modern terms, these natural laws would correlate with what we think of as physics, chemistry, geology, and the other sciences of inorganic phenomena. The most important point to understand about the law of the elements is that the matter it governs is not part of the law

---

2  For a detailed explanation of the Four Elements of Materiality, please see Flavour of Liberation Vol 1, Part 2.

of karma and is not overridden by karma. Karmic law affects the subtle material sphere and not the gross material sphere. So, from a Buddhist perspective, natural disasters such as earthquakes are not caused by karma.

2. **The Law of Living (organic) Matter**. This we might call the natural order of life, growth and decay that we observe in living organic matter. All living matter has an aspect of nutritive essence within it. As part of the expression of life, it absorbs nutrition as part of the growth process and discards waste matter. This natural order governs the behaviour of seeds, plants, sprouts and fruits. Again, this is not an expression of karma, but simply an expression of the natural order of things. Plants, for example, do not have a discrete mental continuum, and so their life is not an expression of volition.

3. **The Law of Karma.** All of our volitional thoughts, words and deeds create an energy that brings about effects, and that process is called karma. Karma pertains to the realm of volition. Volition is that which prompts us to act. This is karma.

The important point here is that the law of karma explains the way that volition becomes a conditioning factor for the way things are experienced. It is important that we do not view karma as a cosmic criminal justice system, and no supernatural force, or God, is directing it to reward the good and punish the wicked. Rather, it is like magnetism or gravity. It functions by discernible laws. One of the ways we can understand karma is by the notion of like attracting like. Those actions rooted in greed or aversion attract unpleasant results in the future when a condition for them arises. Those actions rooted in generosity and kindness attract pleasant results in the future when a condition for them arises.

However, many sicknesses that appear in the gross materiality of the body of organic life, do have their causes in the karmic field and the subtle elements produced by karma.[3]

4. The fourth natural law describes the fundamental truths by which reality becomes manifest. We might think of this as **The Natural Spiritual Law,** (The Law of Dharma). In particular, it describes the truth that 'all conditioned things are impermanent'. Also all things are inherently empty and arise only dependent upon conditions and nothing spontaneously arises without a condition for it doing so. This is Dependent Origination.

5. The final natural law describes **the way that consciousness functions**, and governs the conscious aspect of reality and the process by which we become aware of our experience. Consciousness, feeling, perception and thought processes are governed by this natural law. It explains consciousness to be a discrete process that behaves according to predictable laws. No one person's mind behaves by different natural laws to another's.

Reaching an experiential understanding of how these five principles interconnect takes a deep and mature capacity for insight which develops through the practice of meditation and observes the momentary arising and passing away of both material and mental phenomena and their causes. This is the practice we call Vipassana meditation.

At a superficial level we practise Vipassana, observing the three marks of conditioned existence covered by the fourth law, The Law of Dharma. These three marks the Buddha called anicca (impermanence), anatta (no-self) and dukkha (suffering, or the process by which we find our

_____

3 For a detailed look at this please see 'Flavour of Liberation', Vol.1, Chapters 18 - 28 on the subtle body.

experience to be unsatisfactory). At a deeper level we investigate the process and functioning of all five of these natural laws so that we can reach a profound understanding of the law of causality or what the Buddha called Dependent Origination.

It may take a lifetime of meditative practice to develop a clear comprehension of the dynamic intelligence behind life and the universe, but the point is that, whether we can understand it or not, there are universal laws at work in the background of our lives that condition our experience of it at the deepest level.

Of these, karma is one of the deepest and most profound conditioning factors governing life. The failure to recognise the way in which it functions, and the influence that it has upon life, is one of the greatest causes of the misery that beings bring themselves to, and of the suffering that we encounter.

The tendency to reduce karma to a philosophical idea which we might either subscribe to or reject, has meant that it is one of the most contentious of all spiritual principles. Until we look deeply enough into the energetic processes by which life expresses itself to see it as a dynamic conditioning force within life, we may be prompted simply to reject the notion of it as a violation of our basic sense of entitlement to express ourselves freely in any way that we wish.

The idea that our activities, both within the material world and within the inner world of our mind, deeply condition us to the point where past actions condition present and future events, is quite possibly the most challenging of principles for anyone who galvanises their life around the pursuit of their desires and the fulfilment of those desires in the least inconvenient and most expedient way.

The Buddha himself was quite clear. Our failing to understand the functioning of karma, and the rejection of it as a fundamental principle of life, is one of the main reasons that beings wander for so long in an unnecessary round of suffering. The process of freeing ourselves from suffering is the gradual exhausting of the karmic potential within each of us to come to renewed, suffering existence.

It is on account of not understanding suffering and its causes, and not understanding what it is that brings suffering about, that we organise ourselves in such a way that suffering proliferates rather than diminishes. So far our human efforts to reduce suffering amount to our attempt to bend the world to our will, but we have not yet got very far towards creating a world in which suffering is not an ever-present factor in life.

For, when we come to understand the real nature of things and how karma functions as a reflection of the basic creative process that underpins life, then we gradually come to understand the effect that our actions of body, speech and mind have upon ourselves and others.

As our insight matures we start to experience more directly the powerful conditioning factors behind our lives. With this understanding, our inclination to seek to cut off at the root and free ourselves from those things that are the cause of suffering becomes greatly increased.

The Buddha always was very clear that it is actually only ignorance—not understanding—that is the reason that we come to so much suffering. Jesus was also clear about this. He realised it in his dying moments when he looked out upon those who had betrayed him and persecuted him. Five minutes before he died he was in a state of despair thinking that something was fundamentally wrong, and that God had forsaken him. But in the last moments before his death his insight matured, with the understanding that it was all just ignorance, and not greed and hatred, that was the cause of suffering.

As he saw the confusion in those who had betrayed him and persecuted him, he let go the feeling of despair which, only moments before, had overwhelmed him with the feeling of being forsaken and let down. With his dying words he was able to free himself with the proclamation 'Forgive them, for they know not what they do.'

Sooner or later each of us must start to make a reflection upon what the effect is upon us of the things that we choose to do. How might my actions of body, speech and mind, in the past and in the present, be conditioning the experience I am having, both now, and in the future?

Karma is the volition that prompts us to act. It is the volition that prompts us to act in the moment that impresses upon our unconscious in such a way that it subsequently becomes a conditioning factor in the future, for what we experience and how we meet those future experiences.

Although it is extremely hard to fully understand the complete workings and the dynamic nature by which karma expresses itself in life, it is not hard for us at least to start to glimpse the sure fact that the way in which I react to what happens now, and the actions that are prompted in response to these reactions, impacts upon me in such a way that I become conditioned by it in the future.

This is the most fundamental way that we can come to understand karma. I am angry by nature now, I am angry and resentful of things that happen. The more intense, the more strongly, the more habitually, this anger and resentment arises in my mind now, the more it is accumulated as an impression in my unconscious and in my memory, and the more it is prone to condition my capacity to meet my experiences in the future. This is not hard to understand.

So, likewise, our past accumulation of wholesome and unwholesome mental states (like greed or generosity, ill-will or kindness) conditions our capacity to meet the pleasant and enjoy and appreciate it, and conditions our ability to meet the unpleasant and forbear and tolerate it in the present.

An accumulation of unwholesome states of aversion and craving in the past conditions our ability to meet the present experience in the moment, to the point where we may not be able to enjoy it, or even to appreciate it, because our mind is so heavily smothered by craving or aversion.

A mind that is heavily conditioned in the past by aversion, by intolerance, by anger and ill-will, by craving for this and that, when it meets the unpleasant may become so intensely disturbed by that challenging experience, that it has no capacity to be with it with equanimity. And, without fail, a renewal of mental states of aversion arise within the mind, perpetuating and multiplying and rolling on the causal chain of suffering that is rooted in aversion or greed.

So the arising of unwholesome mental states in the past and in the present is conditioning how we will meet those experiences that come to us in the future. If our mind is too destabilised, or too overwhelmed by anger, aversion and ill-will, by craving, attachment and greed, we will find very little ground that we can land upon in the present moment that feels satisfying, rewarding, or the ground for happiness to arise within us.

And so we see that there is a very poor correlation between the experience of pleasurable things and how happy we actually are. Of course, to experience pleasurable things we are more likely to be happy than if we are consistently experiencing displeasurable things. But unless the mind is wholesome by nature, our ability to meet with the pleasant and find pleasure and happiness in it is hugely diminished.

There are plenty of extremely fortunate people on this planet who are deeply miserable, and many, far less fortunate who have found peace, joy and contentment in their lives.

So this is the first way that we should start to reflect upon karma. We make the effort in the moment to pay attention with mindfulness to the way that we do react to the pleasurable with craving, attachment and grasping; and the way that we do react to the unpleasant with aversion, rejection, anger or ill-will, or intolerance. The first step in cutting the habitual renewal of the cycle of suffering is to pay attention to how we are reacting to what is happening now, regardless of whether we can yet feel how those reactions are conditioned by how we have reacted in the past.

Now all of this will be quite familiar to you if you have spent any time meditating or have done retreats previously. This is not difficult to understand. But perhaps what is just as important, but less easy to understand, is how much good fortune it actually takes to produce a human life that is even relatively free from suffering.

Some of us are extremely fortunate and are not struggling to provide for ourselves the basic requisites that support this life. Others find it much more difficult. This is a reflection of past karma supporting our present experience. It is the past accumulation of merit (wholesome deeds) that provides the ground for the support for this life. This is one kind of karma, the karma that fruited to support the conditions for your life. There are many factors conditioning this.

Most of us, I dare say, are very fortunate human beings: rare amongst humans in our good fortune. So our lives are well provided for. This means there is a stock of supporting karma. One way to reflect upon it is that when life is going well for us it is because our deposit or investment account of good fortune is relatively good, and this will always be because of a past accumulation of merit and wholesome deeds.

But what we may have failed to recognise is how much of that deposit account of good fortune we require to use in the moment, in our ordinary day-to-day life, just to reach a stage where we are even moderately content or happy. In short, far from being of few needs, although fortunate, we are of many needs.

Now it is one thing to have a large and well provided-for deposit account of merit in support of this very life, but it does not matter how large that deposit account is, if it is taking a huge amount of resource to bring you any sense of satisfaction in this life now, you are drawing on your deposit account at an unsustainable level.

The real danger comes when you have become so used to needing so much in order to be happy, that you go through life without investing in the deposit account, expecting your good fortune to continue. When you get to the point where that deposit account is used up and you need so many things to make you feel that life is meaningful, or to feel content or satisfied, what misery will you experience when that ground is no longer supported because you have spent your entire deposit account without reinvesting?

This is the crossroads we have reached as humanity. Most of the history of humanity is the history of beings seeking opportunities to use their good fortune and express it, but with only occasional examples of beings turning their lives to investing in their spiritual or worldly well-being in the future. In fact, at the very time when we experience enough comfort and ease in our lives to turn our attention to service and making merit, we have allowed our needs to continue to rise along with our good fortune, so that our rates of consumption (both material and karmic) have increased alarmingly from one generation to the next.

It is for this reason that the Buddha said that he who is of few needs and easy to provide for is the closest to being happy. He who is of many needs and consumes much in the pursuit of those needs is so far from really being happy.

It is so important that we start to reflect upon this. We as human beings, in this time, in the world that we are living in, have developed such a sense of entitlement that we have come to the conclusion that the basic needs necessary to support our lives are so many and so elaborate, that what could have supported us as a group for countless lifetimes, or certainly many lifetimes, will now barely support us for a single lifetime.

The point at which a being transitions from that point where merit is supporting their life and good karma is fruiting for them, to the point where there is a lack of merit supporting the life and unwholesome karma is supporting them, that is a catastrophic transition that is very hard to bear. It is the transition from these two states, one to another, that brings the most unbearable amount of suffering.

So take stock now. This is the most important reflection that we in our time could be making. There is no reflection that could be more important than this. To what degree are we drawing on our deposit account of good fortune, or simply taking for granted that we will always experience such good fortune, in order to provide what we feel are the basic needs for our happiness? How long can we assume that we can draw on that account at that rate?

It's simple if you look at it like this. He who has £100 in the bank and draws upon that bank £1 a year lives for a hundred years supported by that account. He who has £100 in the bank and draws £10 a year lives for ten years supported by that account. He who has £100 in the bank and draws £50 a year lives only for two years supported by that account. It is not complex mathematics. Why are we not paying attention to the way that we are choosing to conduct ourselves? It is so clear that we are withdrawing karmically far more than we are investing. We are living now a life that stands on the past accumulation of good fortune, but are we sowing the kinds of seeds that will fruit as our good fortune in the future?

When you come to understand karma you understand that you are not experiencing now, in this life, the fruiting of much karma that is produced in this life. Only a small amount of the karma that fruits in this life was produced in this life. Almost all of the karma that fruits in this life was produced in a previous time, and most of the karma you produce in this life will fruit in the future.

In effect both Jesus and the Buddha were trying to tell us the same thing. None of what we materially acquire here will follow us on when we die, the only thing that does is the merit, or lack of it, with which we have pursued our lives. Jesus was not refuting the fact that past actions condition our future welfare, even if he did not explain the mechanism by which this functions in this life and beyond it.

So it is on this ground that we make the reflection: there are beings born in light who are moving into light. They are using their good fortune to sow sweet seeds that will fruit with good fortune in the future. There are those beings born in the light who are not moving into the light, because in spite of their good fortune they are drawing upon their investment account without making new investments, and this investment account will surely, in time, run dry.

So make this reflection on what you perceive your needs to be and whether you perceive them to be greater than they need be, and to what extent you might be able to let go what you do not need or use it for the benefit of others.

Because it is the benefit that your time here brings to others, both now and in times to come, that is your investment in the future. Take heed, because this is a very important time and the way that we meet this challenge in this life will determine how we fare from here. This is the most important lesson, the most important reflection we could make in this lifetime now. And it will determine our welfare in the future.

We may, however, choose to hold the view that life simply comes to an end with our final breath, but even if we do hold that view we cannot hide from the fact that the life we lead will be the basis for what we leave for those to come. Or we might simply hope for a life better than the one we have now. We might even aspire to a higher than human life, like the heavenly life Jesus implores us to aspire to. A higher than human life requires a higher than ordinary consciousness and that would always be rooted in virtue, kindness and love.

It is all too easy to say that the demise of religion in recent generations is merely the result of our feeling of being let down by the institutions that surround them. But it is not just religion that has declined in our lives, but the presence of a spiritual context of any kind. Of course, in our complacency, it is very easy to point the finger of blame somewhere beyond us.

But might we make the reflection that the real reason we have embraced a materialist view of the world and rejected religion, faith and even to a large degree any kind of spiritual context to our lives is because, feeling unable or unwilling to uphold the values that such beliefs ask of us, it is far more convenient to let them fade from the radar?

The Buddha said that the most pernicious of views is the one that assumes that life is just a biological process and rejects the notion that consciousness is the ground for it. Subscribing to such a view that consciousness comes to cessation with our final breath might allow us to feel absolved from all accountability and responsibility for our actions in life.

It may well be convenient to assume that our actions have no consequences, and that the selfish pursuit of our desires and lust goes unnoticed, but let us understand two things. Firstly, nothing goes unnoticed by our deeper unconscious mind, and even though we might be able to pretend we do not feel the way we do, we are constantly conditioned by what is going on within us, even if at an unconscious level.

We can pretend to ourselves that we are happy because we do not like the idea of being unhappy, but we still have to place our head on the pillow at night and be with ourselves. How do you actually feel when you know that you have deceived or cheated someone else, or taken more than is reasonable, in that moment when you get to sit quietly on your own and enjoy the fruits of your labour?

And secondly, if your mind is not peaceful, happy and content now, if you are not kind and generous by nature now, what makes you think that you are suddenly going to become happy and contented, kind and generous in the future, or in another life after this, in a time beyond this? What would make us think that things would so suddenly change if we are currently self-concerned, self-absorbed, selfish, intolerant, impatient, angry, judgemental, jealous and arrogant. What would make us think that we would suddenly change from such a state to one where we are not like this?

This is how we should start to reflect upon the law of karma. We know that sweet seeds sown bring sweet fruit, and bitter seeds sown do not bring sweet fruit. The seed of a lemon does not, cannot, bring forth a sweet fruit. It is not its nature. And when no seeds are sown, no fruit is brought forth at all. You have to choose for yourself whether you are seeking to remove yourself in stages from this cycle of conditioned becoming by bringing to an end the web of karma that is expressing itself through you and through your life, or whether you are simply hoping to improve your good fortune and hoping to find peace, or more peace and happiness, in the future than you know now.

There is no real sign of the merit that it takes to produce a life like this when we pull it apart and investigate it physically. While there are some scientists who claim to have proved that there is no underlying intelligence behind our lives and that it is just a biological process, others are starting to glimpse a deeper intelligence at work, having to acknowledge that it is, as yet, profoundly mysterious and hard to fathom. But even if you are unable to see for yourselves how this life is functioning, we can all at least reflect that it is extraordinarily rare and precious.

The Buddha suggests that it takes tremendous merit and tremendous good fortune to come to such a life as this. Jesus suggests that it will take tremendous merit, kindness and generosity to come to a fortunate life after this. We can all reflect upon how we are using this life, and reflect upon the seeds that we are sowing for our future. We can all try to find in our heart the humility to acknowledge that we may not yet understand. In doing so, instead of seeking to remove the mystery from life, we can look to our hearts instead of our heads to discover the kind of generosity, kindness and compassion that might connect us to those around us and gradually end any feeling of isolation we may be feeling.

Neither the Buddha nor Jesus nor any of the great teachers of the past wished to alarm us with what they shared. They were simply asking us to look deeply into the nature of our lives, and make intelligent reflections and informed decisions about what would be an appropriate way to live in order to safeguard not just our future but the future of those to come. And it is in our hands that these things lie.

It is worth reflecting upon the qualities that do make us truly human, like simple kindness, generosity, compassion and gratitude, and seek to bring them to the centre stage, rather than allow them to become smothered by the pursuit of our ideas or desires. There are many ways that we might seek to mature and not diminish these qualities, and continue to invest in that life account that is the real support to our lives. At every level, surely this is a wholly more positive approach than to blindly hope that things will go our way, or simply seek to make them do so.

For in the final analysis, it is so important to understand that, however powerful and strong an influence upon our lives the will of man may be, the law of karma and the law of nature are infinitely more powerful and they will ultimately always hold sway over the will of man.

# CHAPTER SEVEN

# NUMBNESS IS THE KARMIC RESULT OF IGNORANCE

The Buddha taught that it is ignorance that is ultimately the cause for our suffering, and that our greed and anger, selfishness and ill-will are themselves only conditioned responses that are the result of ignorance. What he means by ignorance is not paying enough attention to what is happening, to the point that we become confused about our lives.

While greed and aversion may be conditioned by our inability to see life for what it is, another significant karmic effect of ignorance is numbness. In effect, if we fail to pay attention to what is happening to us, we gradually lose our ability to feel what is happening.

It has been obvious to all of us who are willing to look with open eyes that the way we have been living for the past 50 years or so has become ever more unsustainable. In a world of finite resources it is a certainty that if we continue to take out more than we put in, it is only a matter of time before those resources that we rely upon for the support to our lives are used up.

It has been clear for some time that we will need to reduce our planetary impact as a species if we are going to even survive, let alone flourish. If ignorance is to not pay attention to what is happening to us, then we have certainly chosen not to pay sufficient attention at the most fundamental level.

And as I have said, the longer term effect of doing that is numbness. The longer we choose to ignore what we should be paying attention to, the more numb we become. The more numb we are, the more willing we are to sanction and tolerate things that are actually causing us suffering. And the longer this goes on, the harder it becomes to reverse its effects.

The more we allow our consciousness to degenerate through ignorance and numbness, the harder it is to reclaim it. And this goes on until there arrives a point where we perceive no way out of the suffering we are in and lack the conviction and energy to bring ourselves out of that suffering. By pretending to ourselves that we do not see and feel the things that we do not want to see and feel, we gradually lose our ability to feel at all.

The more that we habitually refuse to pay attention to things, the harder it becomes to reverse the habit. The longer we smoke after we know it is harming us, the longer it takes to recover. The longer we continue to do anything that harms ourselves or others, the longer and harder it is to reverse the effects of the damage we may have caused. The more numb we allow ourselves to become, the harder it will become to reclaim our consciousness.

The Buddha taught us that, if and when we come to see for ourselves the living truth behind our lives, the experience of seeing this changes the way we function so profoundly that the tendency and propensity to bring ourselves to suffering is cut off. This is what he meant when he said that it is only not understanding what life really is that causes us to live in ways that bring such suffering.

In effect what he is asking us to do is to look deeply into the true nature of our existence to perceive its profoundly sacred nature for ourselves. Failing to find a sacred context to life is one of the reasons we turn to the pursuit of our desires in our efforts to add meaning to it.

Without a wider context and a deeper understanding of what our existence signifies and represents, we simply come to the conclusion that the pursuit of our desires *is* the very reason for our existence. To lose our ability to connect to life at a deeper and more meaningful level is itself one of our greatest causes of suffering.

While we may not be experiencing unbearable levels of hardship or physical suffering, the suffering we experience through becoming numb is capable of causing every bit as much anguish, because it allows us to justify behaviour that we would never sanction if we were really seeing clearly its effects.

For most of us, most of our suffering is mental suffering. Many of us may well not be suffering at the obvious level of physical affliction, but most people when asked would say they are not as happy as they would like to be. To not be at peace, to not be happy, to feel despair, to fail to find meaning in our lives, though not physically painful, causes us to suffer at deeper, more existential levels.

And we may often endure such suffering without recognising that we are doing so. If the Buddha was right in saying that it is seeing life for what it really is that finally launches us upon the path out of suffering, then to lose our ability to see life for what it is, is the greatest suffering of all. And the effect of this upon us over time is unbearable.

Life is sacred, it is mysterious and it is profoundly intelligent. The thread, the current, the field within which this profound intelligence flows is electrical and magnetic by nature, and above all it is conscious. The life current that flows through us, that vitalises us, is electrical, it is electromagnetic. Every time consciousness appears it produces a subtle electromagnetic field. It is within this living, intelligent electromagnetic field that life flows and is expressed.

Thoughts, feelings, awareness, consciousness are alive. They are living vibrations that flow through us as subtle electromagnetic currents. The felt sense of what we are experiencing is actually felt as a living current that flows through us. It is this current of life that defines the quality of our experience. How we feel about what we are doing, experiencing and living is defined by that current of life that is running through us at any moment.

# The Chakras and our Subtle Nerve System

In order to understand more fully how consciousness expresses itself as electromagnetism, we need to understand how our nervous system, and more significantly our subtle nerve system that we often refer to as the chakras, are functioning.

The word chakra means wheel, and with regard to our subtle anatomical system it is referring to the electromagnetic emissions from our body that produce our vital energy field. The chakras are certain areas within that energy field where various aspects of consciousness are expressed.

Our physical nerve system effectively functions as a network of electrical cables through which electrical current passes through the body as a means to carry and convey different signals and types of information. In certain areas of the body these nerves congregate to produce what are called nerve plexuses, for example the solar plexus in the upper belly and the cardiac plexus in the chest area.

As current moves and passes through the various nerves of the body it emits very subtle electromagnetic (EM) fields. In effect every cell in the body emits its own EM field for as long as consciousness continues to vitalise it. While much of the electrical activity within our body is produced by chemical reactions going on at a cellular level, there are subtler currents that are produced by consciousness itself.

And it is these currents that carry the living intelligence that is actually driving our experience of being alive. Without them we would simply be a mechanical system that lacks consciousness and awareness.

In the nerve plexuses of the body these electromagnetic fields become amplified on account of the sheer volume of nerves and the amount of electrical activity passing through them. The emission of this electromagnetism is what we are referring to when we talk about the chakras.

We all know by now that information can be contained and transferred through electromagnetic waves. This is how a radio station, while transmitting at 95.8 FM all day long, can be playing David Bowie one moment and Mozart the next. This is also how all our data is transferred using wireless technology.

Every moment of consciousness produces its own electromagnetic field. When we are angry, that anger produces its own EM field that we feel throughout our body at a much deeper than just mental level. We feel the electrical currents that consciousness produces. This constitutes how we feel: I feel happy, I feel sad, I feel in love, I feel angry, and so on. These are all felt experiences that resonate within our body's overall energy field. And they resonate through our chakra system.

Not only do we feel what we are feeling as fluctuations in our energy field through our chakra system, but we also feel those around us and the atmosphere and ambience of what is going on around us within our chakras and energy field.

Feeling is basically expressed and conveyed, felt and assimilated through the delicate movements of energy and the feeling tones they create within our chakra system. This is the mechanism by which empathy works, it is how we feel the mood of another and the atmosphere of a place. It all happens through resonance.

Although these EM fields appearing within our chakras and in our bodies are extremely subtle and delicate, they account for the multilayered, multi-textured and multidimensional nature of our experience. It is this dimension that brings our experience fully alive as something deeply felt within us, rather than something that is simply going on in our heads and in our minds. It is in these subtle currents that flow through us that we feel the pangs of love when we are close to a sweetheart, or the feeling of pathos when we listen to a moving piece of music or watch a great film. This is also how we know when someone close to us is not feeling well or is upset.

Our subtle levels of perception will be determined by how receptive our chakras are to the ebbs and flows of charge that we encounter. When we are deeply attuned it is like living life through the highest quality hi-fi system. When we are poorly attuned it is like living life through a tinpot mono radio. And when we are numb or shut down we cannot feel what is happening to us at all.[4]

Love, joy, happiness, enthusiasm, compassion, empathy and peace, all of the deepest and most moving experiences that we have, are deeply felt experiences. They are going on at a level that is way beyond the realm of just our mind. They are not just ideas being formulated in our brains, but currents of life moving through us at every level.

This is what we mean by the living energy field: it is the sum total of the electromagnetic radiation that the body emits as an expression of the life currents that are moving within us.

All of our pleasurable experiences are a reflection of varying degrees of coherence within our energy field. All of our experiences of suffering are reflections of varying degrees of incoherence within that field. It is the fluctuations of current, and the relative degree of coherence or incoherence this produces within us, that defines the felt quality of our experience. When we are coherent and well organised, we naturally feel a sense of inner peace and composure and the heart is more open to our experience. The more incoherent we become, the more unsettled we feel within ourselves and the less able we are to assimilate our experience in an open and balanced way. Effectively what this means is that the more incoherent we are, the more distorted becomes our perception of the various experiences we have.

This is the deepest and most fundamental quality of our living experience. How we feel defines our experience far more than what we

---

4 For a more detailed explanation of the function of individual chakras please refer to 'Flavour of Liberation', Vol. 1, Chapters 23, 25 and Vol. 2, Chapter 53

think about it. In a way we could say that what we feel is the essence of our experience itself.

Many of us instinctively pay more attention to the thoughts and ideas that are going on in our mind than the actual felt quality of the experience we are having. But our thoughts are only what we add to the experience with our mind. In effect, thoughts and ideas are always one step removed from the experience itself. It is how and what we feel that marks the real point of connection between us and what we are experiencing.

The vibrations and currents that move through us at the point of contact with the various things we encounter and experience, moment to moment, resonate through us and create in us the feeling associated with that experience. Sometimes we feel settled, sometimes restless, sometimes enthusiastic, sometimes despondent, sometimes we feel love and sometimes anger. All of these feelings are reflections of degrees of resonance and coherence, or incoherence, within our energy field.

How we feel within ourselves at any given time is a reflection of three things:

1. The relative degree of coherence or incoherence inherent within our own life currents and energy field at any given time.
2. What we add to the experience with our mind, i.e. how we react to what we are experiencing.
3. The impact upon this vital field of the ambient energy surrounding us, i.e. the quality of the environment we are in.

A fundamental law of physics states that two energy fields, from any two objects in proximity with each other, will naturally come into resonance with each other. This explains why we feel comforted in the presence of one who expresses tremendous love for us while we are feeling unwell or unhappy.

It explains why we feel uplifted when we walk within the energy of a magnificent, undisturbed forest. It explains why we feel disturbed after a fraught discussion with someone who is angry, depressed or in a state of despair. And it also explains why we can often feel exhausted after a long day in an office filled with wireless technology, or why our sleep may not be as restful when we forget to turn our wireless router off at night. Our feelings are a reflection of the movement of current within us as we come into coherence with the things we experience around us.

So beyond the simple experience we are actually having, there is what we add with our mind. Reactions of anger, restlessness and worry, for example, disturb us at a very felt level. And they do so by disturbing the coherence within our vital currents. Patience, calmness, love, serenity, joy, happiness, create resonance within us and this resonance literally feels good. We feel well or we feel unwell as a reflection of our overall level of coherence. It is as simple as that.

Now, with all of this in mind, let us consider what is happening to us as humans, what has happened to us as humans in the past twenty years or so that has never happened to us before. Because something is profoundly changing at a level that we may only just be beginning to recognise. And yet it is changing the most fundamental aspects of what it is to be alive and of what it is to be human.

One of the things that marks us as humans is our capacity to feel things like love compassion, joy and happiness, as well as anger, despair, grief, worry and anxiety. While we all too easily credit ourselves with our tremendous ability to think, the thing that marks us as truly human is our profound capacity to feel.

So what *is* happening to us as humans that has meant that we are not feeling increasing levels of joy, happiness and contentment as we have entered into an age that ought, in principle, to be more free from suffering than ever before? We have a handle on sickness and disease, we are fed and sheltered, and most of us do not live in a place of social strife, instability or insecurity. We do not struggle daily to provide ourselves with food and shelter. We are intelligent and healthy in general. We live lives of relative ease and comfort. In fact, most of us in the modern western world are more fortunate than any group of humans throughout history. But are we the happiest group of humans in history?

I frequently used to hear talk about how we are coming to this age of enlightenment, a time in which we are all going to wake up. That was the talk that was discussed 15 to 20 years ago. I have not heard it expressed as enthusiastically in the last few years. Why is that? What has happened to the new age of enlightened, conscious humans who were to become the guardians of a considerate, aware, awakened planet? Did we wake up? I'm not so sure that is the case. If I compare us to where we were only 15 years ago, our capacity to feel deeply has broken down, it is broken. We have become numb.

We do not feel what we used to feel, as deeply as we used to feel it. This extraordinary, sophisticated system, through which our deepest feelings are expressed and registered, is breaking. Some of the subtle mechanisms by which we engage in our experiences are not working properly anymore; and things that we ought to be able to feel, profoundly and deeply, we do not feel. And more importantly, we cannot seem to feel what the way of life we are choosing is doing to us.

The little things that used to move us when we were children just do not move, thrill or inspire children in the same way these days. Children today do not experience the same depth of feeling as children used to 20 years ago. And we as adults do not feel what we used to feel either. In the numbness that we are allowing to come over us, we are losing the deepest part of our experience, the sense of wonder and magic, the feelings of empathy and connectedness, the part that makes us truly human.

And why is this happening? It is because we are not taking care of ourselves enough at the most important levels. We are not guarding the real quality of our life, which is the quality of the current that moves through us and vitalises us and defines the quality of how we feel. There is a vital and fundamental part of us that is breaking down. Some of you will instinctively know what I mean when I say this. I am talking about our capacity to connect at the deepest level to how we feel, and be moved and guided by it.

This system that we do not 'see', the one we are just beginning to understand, that gives us this capacity to communicate, to express and to feel, is breaking. We are breaking it. Our solar plexus, our heart chakra, they do not work the way they used to. Even though I had practised meditation for many years, I started to recognise that the subtlety of my perception and feeling was deteriorating as a result of the amount of time I was spending using wireless technology. Having recognised this, I made a concerted effort to repair the damage that I felt was being done. In my efforts I realised that I had to remain vehemently committed to maintaining the integrity of my consciousness at a subtle level if I wasn't going to lose the depth of feeling that I had come to cherish.

I could see that when I listened to a profound piece of music that used to move every cell of my body, I was starting to not feel moved in the same way. And this was because the mechanism that experiences the texture and depth of our experience was wilting and shrivelling like a flower, that it was poorly cared for. I realised that life is always about choices and that we had reached a time where we had to choose to remain conscious, rather than being able to take for granted our deepest capacity to feel.

Most people have no understanding of the violence that is done to this mechanism by which consciousness functions when we sit all day long in a man-made electromagnetic field, or when we are cut off from nature, or when we live and sleep in a sterile environment or with a wi-fi router flooding our room with electromagnetism all night.

The man-made technology that we are in touch with daily does not belong in the field of human consciousness, human perception, human feeling and human experience. What has become our default setting is such an aberration when it is put next to what we are innately programmed to engage in and the depth of feeling we are capable of.

Although we have found extraordinary ways to communicate through our computers and with our mobile phones, our brains have become flooded with dopamine, needing instant gratification, utterly frustrated if we cannot get it. Our capacity to work patiently for something that is deeply valued is decaying. We are reprogramming our operating system, and I would not say that we are reprogramming it for awakening.

Something has got to change. Our children have got to change. We have got to change, or we will become numb, and we will no longer feel things like compassion, gratitude or a sense of appreciative joy or wonder at life. And more importantly we will stop feeling empathy for each other. We will no longer be able to feel these truly profound human experiences that we are capable of feeling if this subtle delicate system of ours becomes broken forever.

It is so important because these are the experiences that make life feel truly meaningful. In their absence life feels lacking, pale and mundane. And if we are not careful it will start to feel meaningless.

We are all going to have to make choices if we are going to reclaim the depth of consciousness that we are surrendering.

This is probably the single most important thing in this book if we can get to grips with it. Because it defines the very quality of the experiences we are having. No matter how hard we try with our meditation, if we do not allow our capacity to feel deeply to repair and heal, we will never end the feeling that something is lacking in our lives.

So now is the time to do something about it, while we can. We have failed to recognise how our pristine natural space and the deep living intelligence that flows through it is becoming violated all the time, everywhere, by the exponentially increasing level of man-made electro-magnetism that we are emitting. But perhaps more worryingly, we may have stopped caring about it. And in our not caring, we continue to sanction the very things that end up bringing us suffering. This is how ignorance works upon us.

These days, a moment of stillness does not provide the refuge or the solace that it should, at times when we simply need to step aside and enjoy some peace and quiet. Many of us are never still these days, and it is very hard to find a place to be still in. We might have to make choices that are not being made by many, in order to go and reclaim that depth of experience that I am talking about.

Switching off your phone, not sitting in front of your television, not spending so long in your car, not spending so long connected to your computer and switching your router off when you are not using it, is a lot easier to do than it is to learn to meditate properly. And a lot of depth will come back to your experience if you just do that.

Technology has brought many conveniences into our lives, but it is in danger of robbing us of far more than it gives, if we do not learn to use it skilfully and in an informed way. In the rush of excitement that comes over us with each new technological advance, there is little sign of what the long term exposure may be doing. Heroin is often described as the kiss of God by those who take it for the first time and there is no sign, at that point, of the damage that long-term exposure causes.

As your meditation matures, you will feel for yourself the effect of these things upon you. The saddest thing is that so few people have any idea of the violence that it is doing to our unconscious mind, our subtle body and our capacity to feel.

I can honestly say this, as someone who has made meditation a major part of my life, that if I were offered the choice between meditating as much as I liked every day but living in an environment that is heavily violated by man-made electromagnetism, or living in nature but never being able to meditate again in my life, I would give up my meditation at the drop of a hat for the chance to maintain the connection to the living intelligence that is actually supporting our lives in the background. I would choose this because I know that it contains an intelligence far greater than anything any of us has yet come to understand, and it is from this connection that our highest inspiration will always come.

So when we ask ourselves, 'Is life really suffering?', we need to ask what suffering actually is. Suffering is to not feel well. To feel well is to be free from suffering. It does not matter what we surround ourselves with in life and what efforts we make to refine the quality of our minds. If we cannot bring our living vital system, that conducts the currents of life through us, into a state of coherence, we will always feel ill-at-ease, and so, experience an inner sense of suffering.

These days we live constantly in such an unsettled state that we simply cannot be with ourselves without feeling agitation of some kind. In many ways this is the worst kind of suffering there is, because it never goes away. Currently our only response has been to seek ways to make ourselves numb, through shutting down our ability to feel, or to remain so mentally distracted that we do not recognise what is going on within us and how that is making us feel.

The Buddha often described suffering as getting what we do not want and not getting what we want. That may be the case when we feel inherently well within us. But these days, all too often we find ourselves still suffering when we get the things we want and when we manage to avoid the things we do not. And that is because we are living with an almost unbearable level of friction, internal conflict and incoherence in the background of our lives. So any path out of suffering these days will need to include measures to reclaim our connection to the deepest part of our heart and our profound capacity to feel.

# CHAPTER EIGHT

# ERASING THE COLLECTIVE CONSCIOUSNESS

O f course it is hard to convey what is happening to us energetically because it is so hard to quantify. But I have no doubt that it will get quantified sooner or later. As I have just explained, we are alive because of electromagnetism. Consciousness is life and consciousness is electromagnetism. The life faculty in this body is electromagnetism.

Simply put, the field that we live in is alive, it is a living field of consciousness. Within this living field we also are all alive and conscious. We are alive and conscious within a unified field of consciousness that is also alive. Now when I worry about something or feel love or joy or ponder my memories, my own discreet consciousness produces a charge, and that charge is alive within me. But it is also alive within that unified living field.

Each of us generates our own psychic field wherever we are and the space around us, over time, accumulates the charge of what has gone on. We often refer to this as the astral field. It is the subtle electromagnetic dimension of consciousness that rests in the background behind the obvious physical appearance of things.

So throughout the course of history, that living field holds the record of what it was like to be humanity, living through what it has lived through. And we add to it all the time. And that is actually at a very deep archetypal level where we get a sense of being part of something, even though individually we may not necessarily have experienced these things or been there at the time. So if you were born and raised in England, there is a feeling of what the land holds, the story of it, the history of it. And you can feel it in you, because it is alive. It is there. And all the experiences that we have shared, and the stories that we have built up, and the ideas, all of that is a huge field of intelligence. And our thoughts are living charges in that field.

When we send a text message, we put another kind of information into that field. It has not got intelligence to it and we do not recognise it. When you put wi-fi on, it puts a charge into exactly the same field, that living field.

It is this unified field that gives us the real sense of being connected, that we are human, what it means to be human, what other people might be feeling in response to how we are behaving with them. Empathy, and all of the subtlety of our lived conscious experience, is alive in that field.

Twenty years ago, there was nothing but television signals and radios interfering with this unified field. So there was a little bit of interference in that field but you could feel that field very strongly. If I was to, say, go back to the time when something significant was happening in your life, somewhere in you, you can feel that, because it is held in the space that you are in, and your sense of identity comes from your connection to it.

What has happened in the last 15 or 20 years is that this field has been microwaved by all this technology, at levels that greatly exceed the natural background radiation in nature. In the same way that when you put your food in a microwave oven and you switch that microwave oven on, it effectively radiates the life out of it. It just becomes dead food. It is just fuel. In the same way our experiences are becoming dead experiences and the depth of feeling and meaning is lacking.

That space that we live in now does not contain that depth of living intelligence it used to, because millions and millions of times every single day everywhere, people are sending text messages, downloading videos and much more. And the more concentrated it becomes, the more intense it becomes.

When we go away on retreat in these relatively remote places in the countryside we can still feel that living field and we can re-attune to it. But in our towns and cities there comes a point where the interference in it is so strong and accumulative that we stop being able to feel it. And at that point we become just body consciousness and mind existing in an incoherent ambient field of electromagnetism that completely lacks the intelligence that is contained in the natural field.

These days there is so much noise in the background going on constantly and it is so much stronger than the subtle resonance of our shared experiences: such as how people felt fighting for what they believed in during the Second World War, or how people felt on 9/11, or how we feel on Christmas Day when we wake up.

The things that add the flavour, depth and texture to life sit in that field, they are alive in that field. And now the problem is that that field is so completely violated by the radio waves used by technology. It is like something delicate playing in the background and then somebody comes and switches on heavy metal music at full volume. There's no chance that you can pick it up. There is not only no chance that you can pick it up, it is wiped clear.

And yet the ambient energy field around us is our heritage as humanity, the shared experience that we have had from the time that we have been organising ourselves as groups and communities and socially sharing our experiences. That is what we share, and from it we get our sense of belonging to something greater. But when that is gone, the sense of what it is that we are doing, or are part of, will be gone with it.

So even if you cannot feel the effects of all this technology, in terms of getting a headache, feeling restless or not sleeping at night, at another level we are feeling it. Maybe we cannot yet feel the shaking in the base of our body that makes us feel so uncomfortable that we have to simply start to shut down. But what will start to happen is that when you are talking to someone, all you can do is listen to what they are saying because you cannot feel what they are feeling. Our ability to empathise and really connect with each other will be breaking down because we are losing our connection to that field where all of our shared experience is held, that astral field, if you like, which is so rich in experience.

Maybe we do not value this aspect of our experience, and it does not feel like much of a loss. But in just twenty years of living in the absence of that unifying intelligence, humanity will seem like a different species, with a different type of consciousness driving us, a different sense of who and what we are.

Although we may not have done the best job of being guardians of this planet over the last two or three thousand years, we have been through what we have been through. The shared experience of suffering during the First and Second World Wars, for example, played a huge part in re-instilling in us a sense of the sacredness of life. As a result, we lived in a period of relative peace, balance and prosperity for some years after. The memory of such suffering remained in group consciousness because it remained alive in the living field of consciousness. The implications of losing this ambient field and all the experiences and intelligence it contains, is enormous for all of us.

These days there are zones and areas where that living conscious field is still there and there is something to plug in to that is more than just what is going on within us at any given moment. If we do not feel that connection to our heart, we would not notice it happening. But when you do feel it you will really notice it. When your heart starts to come back on line again and you start to resonate rather than just communicate, you will feel what is going on.

So the reason that I urge you to try and create space where that degree of microwaving is not going on, and spend enough of your life in that field that is still living, still alive with consciousness, rather than live with noise, with technology, is because in there, in that conscious field, is everything that is beyond the veil of your ordinary perception. And contained within that is the very essence of what life really is. The most sacred aspect of it.

These things are subtle and hard to convey, but I am saying them because I know that many of you will not be aware of them and will not have started to reflect on the implications of our modern technology at this level. At some level most of us will simply be trying to pretend that everything is all right. But we all need to start asking ourselves whether we do really feel alright. And if we do not, are we prepared to do something about it?

We are going to have to make choices, because the consciousness that exists in that field is life. We simply cannot have all these conveniences and it not cost something. We are fighting now for our consciousness. In 20 years the damage will be done. Something will either have happened to put a stop to it, or something drastic will have happened to us. But it is much easier to guard our well-being when we are relatively well, than it is to recover it when it is lost.

This is very important. We may well find ways to survive as living organisms in isolation, having cut ourselves off from what our source of life actually is. But what will be the quality of that survival? What kind of suffering will we then experience? This really is so important. It is probably the most significant thing we face as a species. In some ways it is more important than the question of our survival itself. Contained in all that field lies the memory of humanity's shared experience, the horror that we have been through and learned from, the exalted feelings of grace and compassion and love, and the knowledge and memory that life *is* precious and *is* sacred. All of that is living in that field.

There is no way that a fully conscious being would ever do what we do daily if we could really feel and see for ourselves at the deepest level what life really is. There is no way that any conscious being would ever do to itself or others what we do every day. So where do you think we are going to get the inspiration, the guidance, the impulse to raise ourselves up and be more than that, if we cut ourselves off from that higher level of intelligence?

This is the ultimate example of what the Buddha was talking about when he said that ignorance and not knowing is the cause of suffering. How much suffering do we have to forbear before we are willing to change? It will happen, and it will happen soon. It will get to a point where either everybody has readjusted and we are existing without that consciousness, or we break down at a physiological or psychological level. We depend upon this unified field to remain fully conscious. There comes a point where our man-made emissions smother, or even wipe out, that intelligent living vital field. And that will be the point of real numbness.

The Buddha taught us that greed, anger and hatred are not the root cause of suffering. They are not innate within us, but evolve as conditioned responses in the face of ignorance. Ignorance is to not know, to not pay attention and to not feel what is happening to us. In short, ignorance is numbness. If we see an increase in greed, anger, selfishness and hatred, it will always be a reflection of the degree to which we have allowed ourselves to fall into ignorance and become numb.

The single biggest challenge we face now is the challenge to remain conscious and not fall into numbness. Because that is the only real door by which we will see for ourselves the way that leads us out of suffering. So it is a big issue. It is challenging and we have got to live with it. But always the doorway out of suffering involves seeing things for what they are, accepting them and acting appropriately. Ignorance, numbness and denial of the truth only ever leads to greater suffering in the end.

Remember, over and above all else: life is consciousness and consciousness is life. When consciousness degenerates, life degenerates with it. To guard the quality of our consciousness is to guard the quality of our life.

# PART III

◆

## THE THIRD NOBLE TRUTH: THE CESSATION OF SUFFERING

## BEYOND SUFFERING — THE EXPERIENCE OF AWAKENING

# CHAPTER NINE

# THE SUBTLE MATERIAL WORLD

L et us now look a little deeper into the mechanics and energetics that are going on in the background of our life that we might not normally recognise or understand. In order to really make sense of things, we have to understand principles that are not that obvious when we look at life as a physical body with consciousness arising in it. It is rather like the way that you cannot really understand what a computer does and how it does it just by looking at the package, the box and the components.

You can open it up, you can take it apart, you can look inside, but there is still no way you can understand how it can perform the myriad functions that it performs just by looking at it structurally. It is absolutely the same with a human being. It is not until you understand the information package or the software package that it runs, that you can even start to fathom how it does what it does.

What is more, without that software package it is a pretty useless bag of flesh and bones, in the same way that a computer is just a box of plastic and metal without its software system. In short, consciousness is the software package, and you cannot make sense of life simply by examining it as an organic, physical phenomenon of which consciousness is a by-product.

We seem somehow to have come to such an extraordinarily materialistic perspective on life in our efforts to understand what it is, what consciousness is, what the mind is and what it is to be a human being, by only looking at it mechanically, biologically, physically and trying to understand it logically. In the same way, if we simply examine the computer hardware and try to understand how it operates just by looking at it structurally to see what it is made of, we are not going to figure out how it works.

So in order to understand life, instead of looking at it as a physical structure that grows from a sperm and an egg and forms and becomes conscious, we have to look at it as consciousness expressing itself physically in myriad ways. And you have to understand that the information that it conveys, that expresses itself as life, is a software package, not a hardware package. And then you might start to make sense of life.

When we meditate we start by paying attention to the obvious appearance of things, the structure, the nuts and bolts. That appearance of things is what we are focused on for most of the time in our ordinary consciousness, day to day. Our perception is habitually focused on the appearance of things, which is probably why we have come to the assumption that it is a physical universe that occasionally becomes conscious under certain circumstances.

We start out paying attention to the structure of our body: the hands, feet, arms, legs, heart, lungs, head and so on. When we first start to pay attention, there does not appear to be much more than that there. But as our perception deepens, our awareness starts to open up to, say, 10% consciousness (or 10% awareness) with the remaining 90% unconscious. As we go further we start to develop maybe 15%, 20%, 25% awareness in stages. As we get even more practised maybe we develop 30%, 40%, 50%. That which was not apparent to us gradually becomes apparent, in stages, as the capacity for direct perception develops though our practice.

One of the things that becomes apparent as our field of perception becomes deeper is the subtle aspect of things. The Buddha called it the fine material sphere; I will just call it the software side of things, or the information side of things, if you like. It is that which is going on in the background, which is not apparent when you look at it, but which is actually the cause for all of the functionality that expresses itself as life.

At that point, we begin the journey into the exploration of the part of life that is not apparent to us normally. Even though we have previously struggled to perceive it, it has always sat behind the threshold of our perception, conditioning and governing life in previously unseen ways.

Take how we feel, for example. How we feel is something that is not that subtle, but which frequently fails to make its way into our awareness. If we really pay attention at any time, without any meditation training, we can get a sense of how we feel. How we feel is one of the things that is conditioning our response to life at an unseen level. Just being asked the question, 'How do you feel?' prompts an opening up of awareness in search of something that normally we pay little attention to.

Once we do start to pay attention, we realise that how we feel is a hugely textured and varied aspect of our experience, and one that is deeply conditioning us. We may, for example, have been feeling deeply sad for a very long time, or exhausted, or anxious, or restless, without ever having noticed that this was the case. But the more concentrated we get in our meditation, the subtler our perception of what is going on in the background, the subtler our perception of this information side of things, becomes.

One of the first things we start to realise when we begin to perceive the causal process in the background is that things do not just randomly happen to be the way they are. Once that hidden 90% of our experience that is going on behind the threshold of our awareness starts to reveal itself, we gradually start to get a textured sense, a much more multilayered or multidimensional sense of our experience. We start to glimpse an intelligent causal process behind the coming into being and the passing away of things.

So this we call the subtle material sphere. We are not just talking about consciousness here but the interface between our experience and the knowing of it. This interface is the subtle material world, the expression of consciousness becoming matter. It is not until we start to see that, and start to see it clearly, that we can make sense of how things are. So as we get more concentrated, our capacity for what we call 'wise attention' matures.

If we are able to quieten the mind by resisting the temptation to tell ourselves stories about what might be going on, so that the mind can stabilise itself ever more deeply upon its experience, it starts to see through the appearance of things to the causal process that is going on in the background.

So what do we start to see when we realise that life is not just flesh and bone and the mind? We start to see the first signs of the process by which materiality and consciousness come into being dependent upon each other. We start to glimpse the principles by which they stand upon each other and depend upon each other. And that becomes our investigation: What is going on? How did this body get here? What is this mind that we are entangled with? What are the laws by which it is functioning? This is the subtle material world.

So when you first start meditating, I ask you to start to feel within your body in a way that you probably had not recognised before that you could feel.

The idea that we come to when we look at the body physiologically, is that the brain is the engine-room of the mind and everything goes on there. But the brain is just the top part of our nervous system, an information system that runs right the way through the body. And even the nervous system itself is still hardware. It does not perform any functions until consciousness arises in it. The moment that consciousness stops arising in it, the brain does not perform any of its functions and neither does the nervous system. So it is not until that current of life appears within the body that it becomes functional.

So if we are going to understand how life functions, we need to understand what consciousness does to that body when it arises within it. Otherwise we have just got to take it as a sort of quirk of the universe that this life principle springs into being when a sperm and egg meet. We seem to have been satisfied with that, but it is still rather baffling that it should happen.

It is not until consciousness appears in the body that it becomes more than a lump of flesh and bone. At that point, all of a sudden, it is capable of doing myriad extraordinary things. A human being is the most complex expression of life that there is on the planet, but *all* of nature is an expression of life at one level. And consciousness, appearing and being present within the body, marks the sign that it is still able to express itself as a life-form. The moment it is cut off from that, the body decays.

So it is not our discrete sense of ourselves that is the real intelligence behind our lives. That is what goes on in our brains and makes us not only human, but also extraordinarily difficult to live with. Those flowers in that vase do not have a problem getting on with each other because they do not have a discrete sense of themselves, but they are aware of their environment and responsive to it in the same way that we are.

We as humans have a discrete sense of ourselves, which is wonderful in many ways because it makes life an extraordinary mystery to get stuck into at a personal level. But it also makes us extremely difficult to get along with, because in our individual sense of ourselves we cannot help comparing ourselves to others, and goodness me, how that makes things complicated and difficult.

So this mind of ours arises in various ways within each of us and has a multitude of effects upon us. It is the appearance of our lower mind, that can think and can try and fathom out, 'Who am I? What does it mean that this has happened?' that gets itself in a muddle and makes a mess of life. We often identify with our mind as the essence of who we are, but it is not this mind that marks us as alive.

We live on quite happily, and in many ways more successfully, when we are completely unconscious in sleep and even when we are in a coma. It is extraordinary that we have to spend a third of our life unconscious, so that the higher intelligence behind our life can repair the havoc that our mind creates in the two thirds of our life when we are conscious.

What marks us as alive is the arising of a pure state of awareness, that is not wrapped up with an idea of itself, that does not think, has no opinions or attitudes and does not reject or grasp our experience. It is the appearance of that consciousness within us that fires up or brings online the life process. It brings online all of the functionality that a human being is capable of, including the mental process and the capacity to think. None of the functions of awareness are facilitated by the development of this elaborate idea of what the mind thinks it is doing.

The mind is merely an elaborator of the experience, not the experience itself. It seeks to add to the experience or take from the experience, and in doing so interferes with the flow of awareness through us. I often say to my students, 'When you think, you lose awareness. When you are aware, your mind is completely empty, sky-like and clear.' The mind arises within the body for as long as consciousness supports the life within the body. And the mind, being a function of the appearance of consciousness within the body, breaks apart when consciousness withdraws as we die.

So, there is an intelligence within the liver that has the capacity to metabolise food, there is an intelligence in your heart that knows when it needs to pump a little bit more or less, and so on. In fact, there are myriad functions that are the expressions of the intelligence that is sitting in the background of your life. This intelligence innately knows how to keep it all running and that is not your mind. It is not your idea of yourself and all of your ideas about things. Your thinking mind does not know how to do any of those things. It does not know how to metabolise fat, regulate your autonomic nervous system or your heartbeat or blood pressure. The appearance of your mind is a function of consciousness being present within you and the life faculty being intact. But the real intelligence in your life lies within that basic state of pure consciousness, and it is an intelligence beyond your mind.

I remember when I was younger I had to spend a few weeks in hospital in traction having broken both my ankles. Opposite me on the ward was a young man of 35 who had been in a coma for a few months, and a policeman about the same age who had had to have pins inserted in his toes to straighten them after too many years walking the beat. Over the weeks that followed I watched the family of the man in a coma come and go and attend to him. Although he did not appear to be conscious of what was going on around him, there was a serenity about him. Certainly there was nothing about his presence that suggested that he was stressed, anxious or in any way vexed. The policeman in the bed next to him, however, was drawn and wan from the pain of what he was going through. He was irritable and restless, and looked altogether worn out by his experience.

Then one day, quite unexpectedly, the man in a coma came around. Obviously it was a cause for much delight amongst his family, and although it took him a few days to come around fully and get his bearings, he looked rested and refreshed. When speaking to members of his family, as they came and visited over the coming days, all of them said without exception that he looked well and none the worse for wear for his ordeal. The poor policeman meanwhile, found his entire stay in the hospital totally exhausting and when he was discharged, he really looked as if he had been dragged through a hedge backwards.

The reason I share this story with you is because it highlights the fact that there is a level of awareness that functions beyond our conscious mind to keep the body functioning. It is this aspect of what we might call pure awareness that is the real intelligence behind our lives. We rest upon it when we are asleep and it refreshes and restores us. The life of the man who was in a coma was maintained by it while he was unconscious, so that when he woke up his body seemed to have hardly decayed at all. Although he had bed sores, the nurses told me they were not nearly as severe as the sores of those who were fully conscious during a sustained period of being bed-bound. For all the time he spent resting in bed, that poor policeman looked far from rejuvenated by his time spent on the ward.

The point I am making is this: while awareness itself is the supporting faculty behind our life, the active mind that arises dependent upon that basic state of awareness, actually only serves to interfere with the intelligence within that awareness.

Our active mind arises continuously throughout the day, and even at times during the night when we sleep. This active mind is another expression of consciousness, and it adds to our experience in various ways. It adds to it a flavour, a sense of 'it's me', an idea of what I think is going on, how I feel about it, and how I am reacting to what I am experiencing, while awareness itself merely witnesses the experience we are having, as it is.

Both these two aspects of consciousness, as they appear within our body, produce a subtle material field, a charge of life within you. Awareness itself produces an extremely coherent subtle field throughout the body, and the active mind arising within the body also produces a subtle material field, the coherence of which is utterly dependent upon the quality of that mind.

Every time that mind arises, regardless of what quality of mind it is, it produces within us a charge, an electromagnetic charge. That electromagnetic charge is the field that conveys, that conducts the currents of information that keep us functional. It keeps all of those extraordinary processes functioning which enable you to see, hear, smell, taste, think, move from here to there, paint a picture, sing a song, go for a run, fall in love.

This current of information that moves through us, and the intelligence within that current, that vitalises us, that keeps us alive, that expresses itself as life within us, is governed by the integrity of that innate state of awareness as it appears within you. It is also governed by the integrity of the consciousness that is produced within this mind, that is a fluctuating and conditioned process going on constantly throughout our whole life.

As I have explained, every time consciousness arises within you it produces subtle materiality and it produces a subtle electromagnetic field. And the integrity, or what I call the coherence, of that subtle electromagnetic field defines the integrity and coherence of your experience of being alive and how that feels.

When I teach you to meditate, one of our practices is to sit and practise leaving everything alone and being with everything as it is. I explain how the awareness that is experiencing everything, moment to moment, is like water. Water, when it is left alone, gradually, in stages, becomes mirror-like. As it settles naturally within itself it becomes mirror-like. It is at that point, and only at that point, that it reflects perfectly.

That basic ground of your being, which is a pure state of awareness, always reflects its experience perfectly. This basic state of awareness is not in conflict with its experience. It is not grasping, trying to hold on to it, nor rejecting it. That is the state of awareness that we rest in while we are asleep, and the state that the young man rested in while he was in a coma.

In our meditation we start to gradually enter consciously into that same state, but instead of being unconscious, we are fully lucid and conscious. And at that point, we start to glimpse for ourselves the most sublime experience of peace and luminosity. It is at that point that we understand exactly why it is that being asleep is so important and so refreshing. It is just a shame that almost all of the time we miss it, or fail to recognise it.

One part of our meditation practice is to learn to recognise that the basic ground of our being is that state of pure consciousness. The other aspect of our practice is to bring our lower mind, or our active mind, into alignment with that pure intelligence within that basic state of awareness.

If there is a part of our mind that is always reflecting our experience perfectly, like a mirror, why is it that we are still confused about what is going on within us and around us? Why we are in conflict with how things are? It is because our active, thinking, 'I-making' mind that also arises, moment to moment, as one of the functions of being alive, has become so entangled with its experience, and its 'I-making extravaganza', that it is quite unable to let things be what they are. It has created, to a greater or lesser degree within each of us, a distortion of that mirror-like quality, so that the experience that we are actually having is no longer perfectly reflected into our field of awareness.

If you were to look at a reflection of the moon in a pool of water that was highly disturbed, that reflection would look nothing like the moon. In the same way our experience, reflected in a mind that is highly disturbed, looks nothing like the actual experience we are having. In our own virtual, inner world, our ideas of what is happening to us can become vastly different from what is actually going on. Literally our sense of reality becomes distorted. The greater the 'I-making', the more fixated upon ourselves we become, the greater the distortion in the mirror of our mind.

In this way we start to see how it is. I am not disturbed by what I am experiencing. Physical discomfort is of course unpleasant, but I am not innately disturbed by my experience. I am disturbed by the way in which I react to what I experience, and only by that.

It is not what is happening to me that makes me disturbed. It is how I react and continue to react and have reacted in the past to what has happened to me that has distorted the mirror-like quality of my mind, so that I have become confused and unable to perceive exactly what is going on.

The job we have before us is to untangle that tangled knot of 'I-making'. The tangled knot of this mind that has become so wrapped up with formulating ideas of myself, has placed this entangled knot of conditioning between my true nature and what I am experiencing, to the point that it is so distorted that I do not know what is going on. This distorting of the experience with our idea of ourselves is the cause of our confusion and conflict.

In order to untangle that tangled knot — the charge, the electromagnetic charge, that distorting principle produced by the thinking mind — we have to learn in stages to be with our experience as it is, and stop rejecting it, thinking it should be something else, or grasping it, thinking that it is mine and that I can hold on to it. If we want to rediscover the mirror-like quality of our mind, we have to realise that, whether we like it or not, our experience of life is what it is and we need to learn to be with things as they are. That is what we call equanimity. And equanimity is the axis point of a balanced and harmonious mind.

So if we are going to make any sense of life, we have to start by accepting that it is what it is. Because the moment that we do not accept that it is what it is, we are in conflict with the life we are a part of. Because always and everywhere, regardless of what it is, it is just that. It will not show itself to us in its suchness, as it is; it will not reveal itself in that mirror-like part of our being while the 'I-making' mechanism continues to distort the experience that we are having, reacting to it with craving, attachment, clinging, aversion, ill-will and all the plethora of other responses which mean we are not able to simply be with it.

And of course when we first hear this we think to ourselves, 'But hold on, how pointless and meaningless would it be without that 'I-making' in the middle of it, to make sense of it and to make it all feel worthwhile?' That is the greatest Catch-22 of all. That is the paradox of life. In order to glimpse what is actually going on here, we have to leave everything utterly alone so that we do not distort our perception of it. But in our distorted perception of things, nothing seems to be quite the way it should be, so how can we just leave it as it is?

And this is our mind in all its vanity. The idea that it is all about me and that it needs to have my sense of me in the middle of the experience in order to make it meaningful. That is the confused belief - that my experience is only meaningful on account of my presence within it. That is the ignorance at the beginning of the causal chain of suffering. It was by seeing this that the Buddha freed himself, it was by seeing this that Jesus freed himself from suffering. It is the seeing of this for ourselves, or more importantly, seeing what reveals itself when our 'I-making' finally stops, that frees each of us from suffering.

We have limited our capacity to be with things and have bent to our will not just our experience, but the world that we are experiencing, in our efforts to make it the way that suits us, thinking that this is the way by which we make life truly meaningful. In truth, it does not become truly meaningful until the 'I-making extravaganza' stops being the focal point of our experience and we start to actually engage with life as it is.

It is not until the mind stops adding, stops taking, stops wanting it to be like this and not wanting it to be like that and starts to enter more and more completely into life, that the experience becomes complete and becomes satisfying. With the fading of the sense of me comes the realisation that our experience is not at all dry and pointless and empty without me there. In fact, far from it, it becomes complete and in no way lacking. Our sense of vanity may well take a knock at that point, but our sense of separation or isolation comes to an end.

# CHAPTER TEN

# THE CESSATION OF SUFFERING

The Buddha teaches that the cessation of suffering is the fading away in stages of our sense of self within the experience, so that the sense of being separate from what we are experiencing comes to an end. From within our idea of ourselves, we will all have differing ideas about what we feel suffering to be, and what we think would be its cessation. The breakthrough that the Buddha came to in his own search for the end of suffering was that the only reason our experience appears to be lacking or unsatisfactory is because of the elaborate pantomime of self and all its perceived needs that stands between our true nature and the experience itself.

Reaching this understanding stands upon coming to an experience—whether gradually through the practice of meditation, or suddenly for some other reason (as was the case for Eckhart Tolle)—that impresses clearly on us that the egoic sense of self at the centre of our experience is the root of our suffering, and being freed of it, whether momentarily or permanently, ends that perception of suffering.

Trying to make intellectual sense of this as an idea will always be limited in its ability to impress upon us, and certainly will not be compelling enough to prompt us to reverse the habit patterns of behaviour, thinking and reaction to life that keep us turning in suffering. I have yet to meet anyone who has been compelled enough by the idea alone to successfully dismantle the ego. The point here is that there is an experience that we come to, which, when it happens to us, prompts a choiceless dismantling of our idea of self, and it is this dismantling that we might call the process of awakening.

Awakening from what? Awakening from the confusion caused by our idea of self, to the clarity, relief and freedom from suffering that comes when we experience what remains in its absence.

Being told that self is the cause of suffering is only ever going to be helpful to a point, and indeed making such a suggestion at the wrong time to the wrong person might be taken as anything but helpful.

The role that meditation plays, is to bring us gradually and carefully to this experience for ourselves. The reality behind the suggestion that self is the root of suffering, and clinging to it is the cause, is revealed to us as a deeply embodied truth, rather than a view we might subscribe to or not.

If it really is the truth that the idea of self within the experience is the root cause of our suffering, it is certainly not going to be the case that everyone, simply on hearing this, is going to agree with the conclusion wholeheartedly enough to dismantle the very structure of that ego. It is every bit as likely that some would reject it wholeheartedly as nonsense, and in so doing be prompted to do the very opposite and re-subscribe to personal views that uphold their idea of self.

Meanwhile, it remains a fact that under various circumstances, throughout the centuries, there are countless stories of those who have had an experience which, although hard to convey or even fully understand, has brought a paradigm shift within them that has brought a profound sense of peace and freedom. What is more, it is never the case that such a person has then gone on to reinvent or elaborate further their idea of self, or come back suggesting in any way that the resolution to our problems lies in untangling ourselves at a conceptual level.

It is simply the case that, time after time, however it has happened, through meditation or otherwise, those people who have glimpsed a reality stripped bare of their idea of self, have emerged from that experience not only relieved, but with an unwavering conviction that there is an intelligence behind our lives. And it is living in coherence and alignment with that intelligence that brings peace and happiness, and living in conflict with it that brings no end of suffering.

It will never be convincing enough to just read about an explanation of this process. However, all of us are capable of stopping for a moment and in a moment of inner stillness and calm, honestly asking, from the deepest part of ourselves, whether there is some part of us that senses this to be true at some level, even if, at this point we cannot understand why. And if we cannot go that far, then at least we can ask ourselves whether we honestly feel able to totally reject such a suggestion while it remains a fact that we just do not know.

In the end faith has always played as big a part in the process of letting go as wisdom has. In a world where we have access to all the wisdom we could possibly want at the click of a computer mouse, it is faith, and the courage that it takes to find it, that might be most lacking.

If it were the case that an intellectual understanding of life was the pathway by which we would free ourselves from suffering, then there is something of a conundrum at work in the world today in which we are more informed than ever before, but no closer to being free from that suffering.

As I sit here, there is a robin flitting around outside, occasionally appearing on my windowsill and then disappearing again. He is out there experiencing himself as him, while I sit here experiencing myself as me, and you are sitting there experiencing yourself as you. While it all may feel like a series of separate processes going on at the same time, the truth that we come to experience for ourselves, if we enter deeply enough into our experience, is that the sense of me is actually an illusory process that my mind creates continuously, that gives the sense of it all being separate.

Meanwhile it is a single process at work, endlessly and everywhere. It is the same basic state of awareness that remains as witness to it in me as my ideas of self fade, as will remain in you when yours do too. Right here the universe is a single process experiencing itself as me, while the same single process experiences itself as you. It is a single process expressing itself as the robin outside my window, me here talking and you there listening. The only thing that makes it feel separate is our idea of self. The more elaborate that is, the more separate or isolated within ourselves we feel.

So, as our meditation progresses and our breadth of perception deepens, we start to recognise the unified or singular creative intelligent process at work in the background that is producing the arising and passing of things. It is our failure to recognise and align with this intelligence, on account of our greater fixation on the illusory idea of myself, that prompts us to make choices and behave in ways that bring us to the experience of dissatisfaction.

It is one single process at work everywhere, and it is not differentiating you from me, it is not favouring you and choosing to make you like that and me like this: it is a single unified field of intelligence.

So the more our meditative experience deepens and we land upon this basic ground, the more we experience that it is the same process. The sense of separation between this, that and that is completely gone. It is a single process expressing itself in myriad ways. At that point we are not in the slightest bit surprised that the universe expressed itself outside as the robin, over here as Burgs and over there as you.

When we say that the universe is not in conflict, we are pointing to the process by which things arise. They always arise as a perfect expression of their causes, and the creative process by which they arise is the very intelligence behind our lives. It is this intelligence that we come into alignment with gradually as our idea of self fades.

I sit here now and I pay attention to things exactly the same way as you do and I see the appearance of things. But I am also resting in that place where I feel the causal process for it being there, and I am resting on the basic ground from which it arises as well. So the field of perception is broad, and I am not intoxicated now with the appearance of things because I am just seeing it as life's rich display.

So when we meditate, as we pay attention to the physical process and the presence of our body within that, we also gradually start to see the arising and passing of the mind and the material process.

Gradually we learn to glimpse behind even the arising and passing of things and come to rest upon the basic ground from which it is arising and passing. At that point we perceive these three aspects of reality arising simultaneously at all times: the appearance of things, the creative intelligence behind their appearance, and the basic ground from which they are appearing.

This process of life will continue to express itself as a pure display of the conditions for its arising for as long as those conditions remain, be they the conditions for continued suffering or the conditions for its cessation.

# CHAPTER ELEVEN

# BEYOND THE VEIL OF SELF TO A UNIFIED EXPERIENCE

The Buddha dismantled the idea of ātman, the idea of a permanent soul, teaching instead, anattā, no-self. He is not saying that there is not an intelligent process behind life, but that it is not personal: it is a universal process that we are each having a unique experience of. What he is saying is that this idea of self is created only by the mind, and that this idea of me is groundless when we look deeply into it. Not only is it going to be torn asunder when we die but it is actually falling apart every second, only to be recreated by our dogged insistence and attachment to it.

But this idea of ātman, a permanent soul, the idea of a little spark that sits somewhere within us that is indestructible, is born of trying to untangle the experiences we start to come to when we look behind the veil of appearances and first try to fathom what is going on.

What we actually come to experience when we consciously enter into that place where the mind has come to cessation, is a basic ground, a fundamental ground to all of reality. It is an experience of total luminosity and clarity which, although appearing to be empty, is teeming with potential. This is the experience of an emptiness that contains all things, an alive, living emptiness, if you like, or a unified field of pure potentiality. It is not vacuous and barren, but fully conscious and luminous.

What the original notion of ātman was pointing to was this universal breath of life, this limitless and endless and boundless capacity to be the basis from which all things spring, this field of pure potentiality. We recognise through deep meditative absorption that something rests in the background, behind the coming and going of things, and from which everything is arising. It is this that has been symbolised by the sound Om.

This 'Ommmmmm' that is chanted, is the opening of the heart as it reaches out to touch that universal principle that sits in the background. It is our feeling of connection and that which moves us to prayer and creates a feeling of devotion to the sacred. This is what in Buddhism is called Dharmakāya. And we recognise that this Dharmakāya is the very basis for not just our being, not just my personal indestructible soul, but the basis of all of creation.

But we also come to recognise that while this is the basis from which all of creation arises, none of it actually arises without a cause. It does not just randomly express itself as all of creation on its own. Left alone it rests effortlessly within itself, in the background, as a field of pure potentiality, unmanifest, unexpressed. It takes the creative impulse to bring things out of this unified field into expression.

This creative impulse is what the Buddha called Dependent Origination. At its simplest level, what he was saying is that only with the cause for the coming into being of things, so things appear. Without a cause for the coming into being of things, things do not appear. It is this creative intelligence that we start to recognise in the background, behind the appearance of things, which is prompting them to arise out of that unified field of pure potentiality.

At the most fundamental level, the reason for coming into being was for the purpose of becoming a part of this creative process and experiencing it directly for ourselves, to see what it was all about. It was not for the purpose of showing the world that I am here. Beyond our ego's need to be seen we have a deeper longing, which is the heart's deepest longing to open up and recognise and awaken to what is actually going on here, behind this pantomime of myself that I have become so intoxicated with.

When we start to develop a spiritual context within our lives, as we open more completely to the experience that we are actually having, some beings come to land more upon the basic ground of pure potentiality, or Dharmakāya, seeing that as an absolute principle behind life, calling that Brahman or God. Others come to land more upon the creative principle by which this becomes expressed and call this God, or 'the Creator.'

Regardless of what an individual opens up to and which aspect they first begin to align with, there almost inevitably comes with that an experience of connection and a deep sense that it is sacred, and a growing feeling of devotion to it as such. And so, even within the recognition that there still remains a degree of not knowing, there comes an ever stronger sense that it is known at another level. This is the point at which the view-forming attitude to life is gradually relinquished and we start to allow the experience itself to become our teacher. It is also the point at which the personal will starts to be surrendered to that higher intelligence.

So we see, behind a lower creative instinct that expresses itself through the ego, there is a higher creative principle that is bringing us into being, which is the essence of this life, that we had lost sight of and which we were longing to know.

So as far as mantric sound is concerned, this is the second mantric sound, the 'Ah'. It is the first sound that a baby makes when it emerges into this life, and the sound we all make when we experience anything with a sense of wonder: 'Ahhh.'

The emergence if you like, the coming down, of the creative process into expression, which is the appearance of manifest reality; this third mantric sound is 'Hum'. This whole process of creation, the process by which things come into being, is expressed and symbolised by these three syllables: Om, Ah, Hum.

These three basic vowel sounds are used as an expression of this process of coming into being. The three aspects of reality. The ground, the cause and the appearance. The symbol on the cover of this book also represents these three basic principles.

When we meditate and we enter into a state of absorption or samādhi that goes beyond our sense of self, when we abide deeply in what it feels like to just rest in that empty stillness that remains when the mind comes to cessation, we recognise a light, a luminosity, that is beyond words and that moves us beyond words. And our heart begins to open to that. And what our heart is opening up to when we pray and when we enter deeply into meditation is that unified experience that connects us all. Gradually, as we develop that relationship, our devotion to that replaces, in stages, our devotion or attachment to our little ideas of ourself.

That light of pure awareness and luminosity is never not there. In every moment of our lives, it is resting mostly unnoticed in the background. And it is never not there when we sleep, and it is never not there as we die. We do not recognise it for what it is in our lives because we are so fixated on our ideas of self and the way they attach to the appearance of things. We do not notice it when we fall asleep because we fall into ignorance and lose our awareness, and the same way that we may fail to recognise it in life, we equally may fail to recognise it in death. Fixated upon that which is coming to pass, we fail to recognise the ground from which it is arising.

In truth, there is some part of us that does know this, that has always known it when we sleep, and there is no greater longing in the heart than to know that and feel close to that. When we die, it is the strongest impulse during the life, appearing in the dying process, that leads us on. One who has come to recognise this luminous ground to their being in life, is drawn towards that in their passing. One who has not, is drawn on by the karmic impulses of their egoic attachments.

You have heard me say that this basic ground is a state of pure love. I have not to date read the testimony of anyone who has experienced this saying that it is a barren, dry, or desolate place, or a place of chaos. Everyone, without exception, who has had a fully conscious experience of this emerges from that experience moved deeply by it in an inspired way, even if they find it hard to express what has happened to them. I am sure all of you have recognised, if you have ever come close to it, that it is not a hollow and empty space, it is not a desolate space, it is full of love.

What we see when we look out upon the world, in all its beauty and all its suffering, is that everything we behold, everywhere, is the expression of that love, or the expression of not knowing it. It is the not knowing of that love that is the ground for all the greed, anger, hatred, judgement and pride that beings express, and the coming to know it that brings the suffering thus caused, to an end.

The more intoxicated with ourselves we become, the further from that basic ground of love we get, the more life expresses itself as disorder, chaos and suffering, and the more it takes a concerted act of will to hold it all together. The less intoxicated with ourselves as the creator we become, the closer we get to that profound organising intelligence, the more exquisitely life expresses itself, the less effort it takes to keep it in balance.

On the night of his enlightenment the Buddha said to himself, 'That for which I came here to do, I have done.' He did not make this declaration having invented the wheel, the combustion engine or the microchip, he made it having come to see and enter completely into the way of things, thus ending his sense of separation from them.

Whatever splendours of the highest order there were to be experienced, he had experienced them in his youth as a young prince of the highest good fortune. He had turned away from a life of indulgence and privilege, that most today would long for, finding it empty and suffocating. And in turning away he came to experience the highest expression of love and compassion there was to be experienced. And he experienced these things living the simplest of lives, free of all of the intoxication with sensual delights that he had grown accustomed to, leaving the world unscarred by his presence here when he left. It was having come to experience that and having appreciated it for what it was that it emerged in his mind, 'That for which I came here to do, I have done.'

So think about it in terms of that. I do not know how much faith is going to have to play a part in it for each of you individually. Many people find the way to surrender their ego through a devotional attitude. Without a road map or a way to practise meditation where they can develop a conscious relationship, as the Buddha did, they connect at a heart level, and walk a path of faith and trust that may only complete itself in the final letting go that comes at death.

Intellectual understanding alone may well not open the heart, for it is the experience that humbles us, not the knowledge. The Buddha used to say that one in whom there was too much wisdom and not enough faith tends to become cunning; seeking to resolve things only in their mind they inevitably land upon a ground that upholds their ideas of themselves, rather than dismantling them.

It is faith and humility, in the end, that open the heart. Without it, the heart remains submissive to this mind of ours. The mind is the very creator of our confused idea of self as the creator. This is the reason for coming to the view, 'When I die, it's just curtains. So my time here is to be spent indulging all of my needs and desires.' In answer to that I can only say, you will have to wait and see, for all of us one day will find out where our time here leads us.

So our meditation connects us gradually to this deeply profound creative process that is at work within us. These three aspects, this Om, this Ah, and this Hum, the ground, the creative process and the expression of it, are three things that we gradually learn to rest upon when we meditate.

When you rest upon your own presence, within your own space while you sit, you are resting upon the expression of things as they are. Whether it feels full of friction or whether it rests effortlessly within itself, it is still a pure expression of the causes for its coming into being, which are, for a large part, our personal attachments and desires, but hopefully also gradually an expression of our connection to our higher aspirations.

So the pull, the compression, the compactness that we experience; and the looking left and right and seeking to add something or take something from our experience is all coming from the mind's idea of itself and its need to impress that upon its experience. Your ability to sit effortlessly with yourself is something that emerges gradually over time as you learn to rest in the heart, in the deepest part of the heart, and come to rest effortlessly within yourself the way the rest of nature does. This is when it can reflect perfectly its essence, its true nature, its Buddha nature.

Now of course we are not going to spend our entire lives sitting on the cushion reflecting on our Buddha nature. Hopefully we are going to get off our backside and we are going to jolly well get involved in life, but without being fixated upon the idea of ourselves, perhaps with a greater sense of gratitude and wonder for what we are actually a part of.

So the mountain-like presence within you, like everything out there in nature, rests effortlessly within itself. It is not in a state of conflict. When you sit and you do not rest effortlessly within yourself, it is an expression of the conflict that you are going through, the fighting of battles with yourself, the not allowing things to be what they are.

So that is why we sit. We sit so that we can learn to be here, because not being able to be here is just an expression of our conflict with the universe we are a part of, and the battles we are fighting with ourselves. And all the tension and all the compaction and all the shaking and all the heat that goes on inside us, is nothing more than grasping at, clinging to or rejecting the experience we are actually having, or the experiences we have actually had. So we sit, we immerse ourselves ever more completely, and we become ever more mountain-like in our own presence.

As to that creative principle, well it is the same creative principle at work producing the Buddha that is creating you, the only difference is that the causes for the coming into being are different. One is free from personal attachment, greed or aversion, the other might not yet be. The chain of volition that has prompted us to act now and in the past, is the causal process by which we appear as we do. So we start out sitting not much like a mountain, huffing and puffing, fidgeting, struggling to concentrate upon our breath, but always still emerging every moment from the same basic ground. With the Buddha, likewise, when he first went out to the forest there was a certain amount of toiling, huffing and puffing, and a wilful effort put forth to free himself from suffering before he finally surrendered and let go.

Eventually we all come to know the same basic ground, and love as the original and final cause for the arising and the coming into being of things. At that point our suffering comes to an end. For as long as we do not know that, or remain separated from that, we will continue to experience suffering.

So where this all lands is this: what appears here in the universe is always and everywhere an expression of the causes for it. When love is the cause for the coming into being of things, then love gets expressed. When selfishness is the cause, then selfishness gets expressed. So the universe always expresses itself perfectly and none of this is ever out of place.

Everything always expresses itself perfectly the only way it ever could, and so there is never really a hair out of place. Greed expresses itself as greed, anger as anger, selfishness as selfishness, love as love and ignorance as ignorance. So as we gradually surrender our fixation on ourselves and our obsession with our selfish creative desires to more altruistic creative urges, slowly a higher principle, a higher consciousness gets expressed through us, and slowly in that way, and only in that way, do we come to see what we are truly capable of being.

So that which is still beyond you is reached partly through coming to know, and partly through your devotion to what is still to be known. This is the devotion to one day find within you your own expression of that which you most highly aspire to in the purest part of your heart. Our hope is that one day that which we pray to becomes expressed through us. That is our devotional attitude. It does not ask for any personal preference or gain, it is not expecting any help out of our predicaments, it is asking only for the inspiration and the courage to stand upon its conviction and not give up.

Om, Ah, Hum. When we chant that 'Ommm Ahhh Hummm', we are watching, meditating upon and contemplating that process by which pure consciousness expresses itself. And we are hoping that in this 'Ahhh', this longing in our heart, becomes purified enough that this 'Hummm' becomes an expression of our true Buddha nature.

How wonderful.

# CHAPTER TWELVE

# THERE'S NOTHING LACKING

As we start to turn up more completely within our experience, as our sense of self fades from the foreground and as our sense of separation from what is going on around us likewise fades, so the deeper, more meaningful and moving feelings and textures to our experience begin to emerge. The things that we may have started to feel were lacking, gradually cease to be, and gratitude, appreciative joy, compassion and love for life, and eventually a total, unconditional, accepting love for it, come to maturity within us.

Before this point, while we remained so distracted by ourselves, our efforts to experience these things were limited by our personal need for the universe to fit my idea of myself. In short, we were unable to unconditionally allow our experience to enter into our awareness without filtering it.

But as we let go our fixation upon ourselves, our experience of love for ourselves transforms from one of vanity to a deep experience of gratitude and deep appreciation for the fact that we are even alive. Unconditioned by our idea of ourselves, with all its attachments, with all its clinging, with all that it rejects, our experience of love, compassion and appreciation become boundless.

And this process works itself through, not at a level of ideas. It does not come about because I understand the idea of needing to be out of the way. It happens at a deeply embodied, energetic, felt level. The felt, experienced quality of our life, moment to moment, becomes complete when we leave our experience alone. Because at that moment, the impedance that this 'I-making extravaganza' has packed into our system, is gone. And the conflict that we experienced on account of this impedance has gone with it.

And it has not gone because things turned out the way we wanted them to. The conflict has gone because we are now completely and utterly able to be with what is happening to us. And we realise that the universe was never in conflict. The conflict was all an illusion that we created, which was just part of this 'I-making extravaganza' that went on in our mind, as a figment of our imagination.

And that is a deep, lived experience that comes about in stages at an energetic level. It is a transformation in the way in which life is expressed through us. There will not be much of a change in how it looks, in the same way that there is not much of a change between when you are alive and when you are dead in how you look. But at a hidden level, at that subtle level, in the software side of things going on in the background, that we had not previously noticed, everything has changed so profoundly. We are not even running the same programme any more.

That limited intelligence of mine that I imposed upon my experience, that did nothing but impinge upon it and create impedance, has gone, and that boundless pure intelligence that always was desperately trying to support my life, and all life, all the time and everywhere, is now expressed within me. That is a very, very profound change, and brings with it an enormous sense of relief.

And when you are living the experience of that, you will know that the universe is not in conflict. You will know that it is pure intelligence and the only reason that it did not feel like that was because I put myself in the way.

So something very profound starts to happen to us that is very difficult to fathom when we start. When we start letting go our conditioning and start creating within ourselves a willingness to be with life, as that willingness to be with it matures, the conflict that we have been experiencing fades in stages.

That is what happens to us when we do what the Buddha did, what every other being that has freed themselves from suffering has done. That is how mechanically and energetically the process of transformation comes about, and brings on the lived experience of the freedom from suffering. And it is an expression of life. It is life, lived and expressed; and it is worked through at that level. It is not worked through in your mind as an idea or a resolution that you are going to come to, which is suddenly going to make the universe that you have been fighting with make sense.

Before this point we might sit on our cushion and do our meditation, and as our meditation starts to mature, almost every day new ideas appear in our mind. We rewrite our world view, we put a bit into our 'how

I think it is' spreadsheet here, and we take another bit out there, we move this bit around trying to crystallise our ideas into a coherent vision of awakening. But the process of awakening is not something that is resolved in our mind. Rather it comes upon us within our experience itself when our mind stops long enough to leave the experience alone, and the such-ness of it, of what was always there, reveals itself.

Love is not an experience that goes on in your mind, is it? It is a much deeper, a far deeper experience. So is compassion. It is not an idea that we grapple with, it is a deeply embodied, deeply felt flavour of our experience. And it is expressed, to a greater or lesser degree, dependent on how smothered that experience is by our idea of ourself.

Awakening likewise is an experience, it is an experiential process. Life is an experiential process. Within it, mind is a part of what we are experiencing, but do not get lost in it, it is just a rabbit hole. Whatever we are capable of dreaming up, between us we have probably dreamed up. And it adds to the texture of what we are all experiencing as a group, but life will not reveal itself in its nakedness, as it actually is, until we remove that, or until we allow that to fade. Maybe in stages, not suddenly but gradually, as the I-making and storytelling stops impinging upon the experience that we are having, we see it for what it is.

I am trying to express this in terms of the principles that you can resonate with as being at work within you in your life. This is why I am not trying to teach Dharma as Dharma by the book. I am trying to convey it with a wetness that you can relate directly to, as a living principle or living Dharma at work within your life, at an experiential level. This is the only way that real wisdom can mature in us, not through mere understanding but through experience. Wisdom is that insight that lands within us and opens our mind in a way that helps us move forward. But it is very difficult to express.

I am trying to point out the signposts that we are looking for within our practice that are going to reveal this process to us experientially, in stages. Because that is the bit that will actually transform us. The idea will not transform us, even if you subscribe to everything that I have just said, but seeing it and experiencing it for yourself, will.

# PART IV

◆

# THE FOURTH NOBLE TRUTH: THE PATH THAT LEADS TO THE CESSATION OF SUFFERING

## FROM BONDAGE TO FREEDOM—THE JOURNEY HOME

# CHAPTER THIRTEEN

# THE QUALITY OF YOUR LIFE REFLECTS THE QUALITY OF YOUR MIND

I explained previously how, in our pursuit of happiness and the cessation of suffering, there are those who progress swiftly and painfully, swiftly and painlessly, slowly and painfully, and slowly and painlessly. What is the reason for this? One key factor will be the karmic support behind our lives, which is our accumulation of past merit. The other key factor is the inherent quality of our mind. The Buddha identified ten positive aspects of character which, when brought to maturity within us, determine whether our progress out of suffering is swift or slow, painful or painless.

Although most of us have a tendency to look outside ourselves for the causes of our suffering, when we actually pay attention we discover that for anyone who is not living a life of abject misery, most of our suffering is mental suffering, and most of our karma is mental karma.

Karma, as I said earlier, is the volition behind our actions of body, speech and mind. By actions of mind we mean thought processes. As our idea of ourself proliferates, it prompts ever more elaborate attitudes and reactions to the world and what we experience therein. The way we experience our mind, i.e. our mental feeling, our state of mind and so on, is an expression of mental karma.

Many of us continue to feel we are suffering from things that have already come to pass long after the event itself is over. For example, you were once cheated by your business partner, and years later you are still suffering from resentment, and on account of that you feel unable to trust anyone. It is clearly the case that you are not currently being cheated by anyone. No one is causing your suffering now but you. Almost all of our suffering is going on in our mind, as an inability to be with our experiences when they are happening, and our inability to let them go as they pass.

As a meditation teacher, I meet so many people who are suffering almost entirely in their mind, while on paper their life looks to be most fortunate indeed. This suffering is largely produced by what we call pride, which is the comparing of ourselves to others as better, same or worse, or comparing our experience to how we think it should be as better, same or worse. This taking everything so personally is the cause for our not letting go of things that have, in truth, already come to pass.

Every time we are challenged by life we have a choice. We can point the finger of blame at our misfortune and, on account of it, find an excuse for not getting on, or we can accept that it is what it is and get on, in spite of our challenges. Our challenges are our invitation to evolve; a chance to find something within ourselves that might otherwise be lacking. It is up to us whether our challenges are our undoing or the making of us.

One who is not sick, not struggling for the requisites to support their lives, or overwhelmed by the effort to do so, is not struggling on account of external things, but struggling internally in their mind. The problem is that our ideas of what we want and need and how we think things and others should be are so elaborate that it takes tremendous energy, resource and effort to uphold and fulfil those ideas. This is like trying to cover the world in carpet so we do not stub our toes. It cannot be done. What we need is a sturdy pair of walking shoes. Those sturdy shoes are the base of our mind, or the basic makeup of our character.

So when you see how things are, your mind will be free of suffering. When we truly see how things are and the process by which they come to be that way, the mind arises with one of only four responses. The first thing that happens is that we gradually stop being in conflict with things and come to a state of acceptance, which we call equanimity. This equanimity is the state that neither rejects nor grasps the experiences or objects that we encounter.

Once equanimity has arisen, and only then, there may thereafter arise in us three further responses. These are love, compassion or appreciative joy. This illustrates a crucial point regarding the functioning of our minds. And that is this: all of the truly noble qualities of our mind — love, compassion, gratitude, appreciative joy — only arise when we are not in conflict with, or clinging to, the experience itself. This is because both aversion, which rejects, and attachment, which clings, shrink the heart base in a way that prohibits the arising of such positive mental states. What this means is that our mind fails to reach a wholly positive state until it has reached a state of complete acceptance.

We can see how even Jesus went through this process in the minutes before his death. Five minutes before he died, he was confused, he looked out upon the world as he hung upon the cross and saw only hatred, anger, greed and fear. Unable to see beyond that he came to a state of despair. Feeling that he had been let down he turned to God saying, 'Why have you forsaken me?'

Only in the final moments of his life did his insight reach total understanding and thus come to a state of complete acceptance, as he looked again upon those who persecuted him and those who betrayed him. No longer seeing their hatred, greed and fear as the cause of his suffering, he saw, as the Buddha saw, that all of these things are only ever rooted in confusion. And in that moment he freed himself from suffering with his final words, 'Forgive them, they know not what they do.'

The truth is we really do not know what we are doing. We do not know how we might be sowing the seeds of our future suffering with the way we meet our experiences now.

So, the Buddha's path, the Eightfold Noble Path that leads to the cessation of suffering, is the path that teaches us how to see beyond the veil of appearances to the truths that lie behind them. It teaches us how to 'see into', which we call insight. Insight means to see into, it does not mean to sit down and have a jolly good think about how things might be. And it is a faculty of the mind that matures gradually as our ability to concentrate and pay attention develops. That is one of the reasons we practise meditation — because it teaches us how to see into life, and it is that 'seeing into' that transforms our mind.

However, in order to get to the point where we can see what we cannot see now, we are going to need to put forth a certain amount of effort to clear, what the Buddha called, the dust that is in our eyes. The dust in our eyes is the idea of ourself that we are entangled with and all the attitudes and habit patterns of mind that it has prompted.

The Eightfold Noble Path itself breaks down into three aspects. The first is the restraint of conduct and the refinement of character that is necessary for the mind to become calm and stable, prior to the development of concentration and insight. Once concentration and insight matures, the mind begins to purify itself, but prior to that point, restraint in conduct and effort are required until we can actually see for ourselves.

And while we are working to develop this capacity to see, there are certain basic faculties of mind, or what we might call refinements of character, that help expedite the process. The Buddha called these faculties pāramīs, which means perfections. What he meant was that it is the perfecting of these qualities within us that ripens our mind, so that liberating insight can arise.

There are traditionally ten pāramīs, but of course there are other noble qualities of mind beyond these. The point is that once these are mature in us, the other noble qualities will follow on. It is worth taking some time here to explore the notion of refinement of character and the ten pāramīs in particular. It is fair to say that any effort to develop meditative stability without making the effort to restrain the mind and develop these qualities is actually an act of vanity. So this aspect of refinement of character is absolutely at the heart of any genuine spiritual path and practice.

# The 10 Pāramīs:

## Generosity

Generosity is the first pāramī. Generosity is the willingness to give, or to share. We mean generosity of spirit, as opposed to stinginess, or the inability or unwillingness to share or give. Now our good fortune is the result of generosity in the past. So when we are well provided for in the life, it is because our pāramī of generosity has been strong in the past. One who has generosity shown towards them and has their basic needs provided for them, would have done things that helped provide these requisites for others sometime in the past.

When we develop our pāramī of generosity by providing for our children, we create the grounds for being provided for by our parents in the future. When we give or share what we have rightfully earned for the benefit of others, we create the ground for acquiring our basic needs with relative ease in the future. When we fail to support those in our care, be they our children or parents, we sow the seeds for lacking that support in the future.

When we earn our livelihood with relative ease and do not reflect that this is the fruiting of our good fortune, and instead feel proud of ourselves and squander our good fortune in self-indulgence, we fail to renew the field of merit that has supported our lives and so are unlikely to come to such good fortune in the future.

Generosity is the first pāramī because when we have little we can still find ways to give of ourselves, be it our time or energy. When we are in a state of real confusion we can still find ways to give. To be of service, helping, doing something that is for others, that is generosity of spirit. Performing acts of kindness and generosity is the fastest way to lift ourselves when we are feeling stuck or depressed or shut down, because it starts to open our hearts again and takes the focus off ourselves.

## Virtue

The second pāramī is virtue, which is understanding what is appropriate behaviour and understanding what is not. It is morality. At its most basic, it is unwillingness to harm oneself and unwillingness to harm others.

This unwillingness to harm ourselves or others acts as a tremendous protection, because when we do things that are harmful, not only is that unwholesome in the moment, it opens the mind-door through which all our past unwholesome karma can fruit. Karma only fruits through the appropriate mind-door for it. When you are feeling expressions of love, your unwholesome karma associated with past actions of aversion and anger does not fruit unless it is really strong. But when you are feeling anger or you are feeling greed or craving, your unwholesome mind-door opens and the past karma connected to these things can then start to fruit.

This is why getting really intoxicated is so potentially dangerous to us, because we may normally have quite well-composed minds where we know we would not normally do things that would be reckless, inconsiderate, hurtful or harmful. But in a moment of forgetfulness we might do something that we later would regret.

Not only in that moment might we do something that we would regret, we may open the mind-door that normally would not open within us because we are reasonably well grounded in virtue. And at such moments our past negligent karma may fruit for us. I have heard horrendous stories from  people coming to see me who have got themselves into the most unimaginable state through getting intoxicated, getting into such a state of forgetfulness that the whole chain reaction of karma starts to fruit, when previously there was no sign in their life that it could possibly have happened.

So mindfulness, which is awareness of what we are doing, is our protector. When we get really intoxicated, we have lost our mindfulness and if we get really intoxicated we can really lose our way. Here is an example:

One friend of mine, whose life was going absolutely swimmingly, was travelling around Australia. He got really high one night and passed out on the steps of the town hall in Sydney. He woke up about three days later in a squat with a syringe in his arm; he had been injected with heroin. Within weeks he had a heroin habit which he then found himself completely lost in for a while. He completely lost his way and his life became a total nightmare. He did not know where he was, and he could not get himself out of there. He completely lost all sense of perspective and all control over his life.

From where he was, having the time of his life and loving it, he reached a point where he was in no way able to pull himself back together. He came on retreat about two years later having been in a total mess. On that retreat I gave him some healing, and the energy that was smothering him was so dense that, had that not been removed, he probably would have been living in a stupor for the rest of his life. During the retreat he worked through that energy and cleared the karma associated with it, and today ten years later he is flourishing, loving life, with a successful business and great family.

I have seen a number of cases like this over the years that I have been teaching. The point being that all of that unfortunate karma fruited in a moment of negligence, when before that point there was no sign of it. He went out and got drunk one night and passed out on the steps. Then all of a sudden it just spiralled and spiralled, and then his mind became unstable, and from there he quickly fell into a state of total despair. In the end he could no longer help himself and it took an intervention to get him through it.

Even to receive the help that we need when things are tough requires good fortune. Even that is the fruiting of fortunate intercepting karma. I have known a number of situations like that, where people have got themselves into an horrendous state. You might be out having a good time and then suddenly you just do not know what you are doing and then 'bang', it all gets really messy.

So there is a point of forgetfulness where, if you have such messy karma in the background, you create the opportunity for it to fruit. This is why we learn restraint in our conduct while we are working to cut off at the root our remaining tendencies to cause suffering. When you have that ability to restrain yourself, there is a point beyond which you would not go that is actually your protection until your mind is purified of any tendency to go completely off the rails and get yourself into a terrible state.

So that is the reason to be careful with regard to intoxication. How much suffering is caused by that, do you think? How many children born of intoxicated lust? How many marriages or relationships broken while intoxicated, in ways that in a sober state would never have occurred? The balance of a human life is maintained by our innate capacity of mindfulness. We so quickly lose that balance when we lose our mindfulness.

Let us return to this idea of 'unwillingness to harm oneself and others'. So if you are battling with greed, or you are battling with anger, but your virtue is strong, your unwillingness to harm others is strong, you will not be prompted by greed to pursue your desire at all costs, at the expense of everyone and everything. If you are furiously angry but you have a sense of virtue, you would not be prompted to pursue your anger or ill-will at the expense of everyone and everything.

So our unwillingness to harm marks a point beyond which we would not go, and it is really important to reflect upon that and try to generate some conviction behind it. Because we might think that there are certain things we would not do, but then if craving arose really strongly and we absolutely had to have something, we might be willing to set aside our willingness to harm.

Now that happens a lot with regard to lust, in the way people pursue each other, in an uncontrolled way, when someone is in a relationship or meets another who is. If there is no restraint to our greed, craving or lust, then we are willing to create no end of suffering in the pursuit of our desire. And on the other side, when we are really angry with somebody and get really bitter, this is our own mental suffering on account of anger. But if we go beyond that, to point where we would want to see that person harmed, that is when it really gets messy and we start to create real misery for ourselves and others.

When there is no willingness to harm others in spite of how you feel, then your greed and lust or your anger and hatred will only go so far, and it will not go beyond that. This is the importance of unwillingness to harm self or others. The Buddha called the two unwholesome states of willingness to harm 'lack of moral shame' and 'fearlessness of wrongdoing'.

The single greatest protector of our mind, while we are still battling with our craving and really struggling with our anger and aversion, is what we call ahimsa, or harmlessness. When there isn't anything we would do that would prompt us to either harm ourselves or harm another then we are protected from our greed and aversion.

When this harmlessness is not present within us, then things really start to degenerate, even to the point where we would harm others and ourselves doing things we believed were right. So virtue is our protection from coming to misery on account of past karma and creating renewed misery for ourselves and others.

## Energy

The next pāramī is energy, vitality, or vigour. Now this is extremely important. It takes tremendous energy to raise your levels of mindfulness, concentration and consciousness up to the point where you can see through what is apparent to what is going on in the background. It takes tremendous energy to find restraint and determination and patience, particularly in an environment now where everything is geared towards very swiftly getting what we want.

In many ways it does not require much energy or tenacity to get what you want now. Almost everything you desire, you can have as soon as you want it. But happiness is not something you can have just because you want it. The end of suffering and the end of mental affliction, and the end of physical pain, is not something that happens just because you want it.

It takes tremendous energy to raise yourself up and change the direction of your life because, remember, your life now is the result of past choices, and it has a lot of energy and inertia behind it already. So to realign that, particularly if it involves a change of direction, takes tremendous energy. And this vitality needs to be looked after so that you have enough to skilfully move through life without it being an exhausting struggle. We consume so much vitality with our mental pursuits.

I have explained how 90% of our karma is mental karma. It is likewise very easy to consume almost all of our energy with our mental pursuits, with the way we obsess over things without end. A lot of our vitality is haemorrhaged through excessive mental activity but as the mind cools down, a tremendous amount of energy comes back to us.

We also lose a tremendous amount of our energy through excessive sexual activity, although this is not as much the case for women as it is for men. The sexual drive is a very deep, instinctive drive. It is very, very difficult to temper and remove the lust from it and to moderate it. Most of the time the only moderation comes from not actually being able to have sex all the time.

This is why restraint is very important, because to surmount our lust to the point where we are not driven by it takes great discipline. If we look around the world, and we look at the causal factors by which it came to be the way it is today, most of what we see expressed around us in the world is the result of lust, in one form or another. That is quite a staggering thing when you see it clearly. The display of things, and the way in which the human world presents itself now, most of it is the display of, or the result of, lust. It is a very strong and prolific energy, and it takes tremendous restraint to not be totally driven by it.

Lust is not something that is easily surmounted, but to learn to claim back some of the energy that it pulls from us returns a tremendous amount of vitality back to us. So there is a balance. When you restrain the obsessiveness of the mind, it stops consuming vitality, and you get a tremendous amount of energy back. When you temper the sexual drive so that it is not pulling on you all the time, you experience a significant increase in vitality that becomes available for other aspects of your life. Actually, it is not until our creative force and our mental force stop running riot and the sexual drive is tempered, that the central channel5 opens. When this happens, it brings about a quantum shift in the amount of vitality that we have.

This is the process of internal alchemy that brings about the transformation of desire into a positive vital force that supports our lives. It is this that we call spiritual energy. Without it, our mind is scattered and messy, poorly organised and we get exhausted by the daily round.

In truth, we get our vitality from two aspects of consciousness. There is the vitality we get from being plugged into source, i.e. our natural environment and the vast field of energy that it contains. And there is the vitality that is produced by the volitional aspect of our mind as desire, which is karma. Each of us will generate our total level of vitality from a combination of these two sources.

Some of us are very desire-driven but may not be that connected to the universal energy field around us. Others may be less driven by desire but more plugged in to the universal field. Problems arise when we lose our desire for the things that have driven our lives — ambition, motivation, even greed and so on — and fail to connect to source at a deeper level. This is one of the main causes for various degenerative conditions like chronic fatigue and even depression. In a similar way, when one who is not driven by desire but derives their vitality from connection to nature, for example, finds themselves in an environment where they cannot make that connection, they will also experience a

---

5 The central channel is called suṣumṇā nāḍī in Sanskrit and refers to the energy pathway through which pure awareness flows. For a more detailed explanation please refer to 'The Flavour of Liberation', Vol. 2, Chapter 53.

significant drop in their feeling of vitality. This likewise can cause either a chronic feeling of physical exhaustion or mental depression.

So energy as vitality and vigour is very important, because it takes tremendous energy just to sit there and try to break through dullness, sloth, laziness, restlessness and ignorance, and develop real concentration and mindfulness. But until we do, we cannot start to see what is actually going on or start the real process of transformation beyond the initial refinement of character.

## Patience

Patience is the quality of tolerance and forbearance, of being able to allow things to come about in a timely way. It overcomes our growing need for instant gratification. Some things in life we have to work for patiently. We cannot always expect to get what we want just because we want it. Many problems that arise in life will not get resolved quickly, they take time and perseverance, forbearance and patience. Often these things that do not suddenly happen can turn out to be the most precious of gifts.

In a modern world where we are growing used to getting what we want quickly, it is easy to develop a sense of entitlement, stamping our feet or getting in a huff when things do not go our way. But with things that are precious and really of value to us, it is worth putting forth effort and being patient.

In nature, when a seed is planted it takes time for it to bring forth fruit. We may have lost touch with this simple truth and become frustrated by things that do not reward us instantly. Life is so much more than an expression of our personal will, and there are deeper currents at work within the fabric of life that we need to be aligned with if we are going to maintain an inner and outer balance. Patience includes the attitude of giving things the time they need to come to fruition and completion.

Unfortunately, many of us have become so used to being able to instantly gratify our needs that we develop real stress when things do not go our way. We want a book, we order it and it arrives the following day. We want something specific for dinner, it is at our fingertips. It is easy to forget that some people still have to walk half a day just to get clean drinking water. Even being able to buy things on credit instead of saving up until we can afford them begins to diminish how we value the things in our lives.

This is particularly important in relation to children. The quality of mind that follows us throughout the life is laid down largely as we grow up. Often, after a retreat, a parent will ask me what is the best thing they can teach their kids. I will often suggest that they give them things to do that take time, that they do not complete quickly, that they have to walk away from and come back to. And the second thing I suggest is that they teach them to do things where they have to really pay attention and concentrate.

For example, when you take them camping, the fact that it's going to take all day to build the camp and set it up, get the fire sorted and get the food store done and get the tents up, this is not only going to take time to do it, but it is going to take perseverance and concentration and application. Many of the ways kids entertain themselves these days are geared towards hyper-stimulation and instant reward. This is one of the reasons behind the growing occurrence of ADHD.

To teach patience and concentration to children in their early years is such a blessing. For them to learn that we cannot have something now, just because we want it, prepares them for the life ahead. In a world of constant stimulation and instant gratification, patience is the much-needed antidote. Those who are patient are, by nature, far more settled and peaceful within themselves than those who expect always to get what they want.

Try to take some time to reflect on your own pāramī of patience, and see if you can recognise where a lack of it is limiting and hindering you, and where your life feels enriched by the instances when you have found patience. Think about including things in your life that will bring reward on account of the patience you find. Reflect also on the relationship between patience and intolerance, and see if you can identify where a lack of equanimity and acceptance of people and things in life is underpinned by an undercurrent of impatience.

## Determination

Determination is the application of energy and the willingness to stick at things. It overcomes laziness and the feeling of not being able to gather energy to do things. It is the sustained effort and resolve that is required to see things through. Determination arises when we encounter hindrances and we do not give up in the face of them. A huge amount of suffering is caused by laziness. There is nothing more withering than knowing what you need to do and not doing it. That is called indolence.

It is one of the most insidious weaknesses of character and because of it we continue to come to suffering even when suffering is no longer necessary. We see what we need to do, and yet we continue to suffer because we cannot find the conviction to act upon it.

The Buddha had worked for six years trying to free himself from suffering, and yet he still had not succeeded. Having almost died from practising in an unbalanced way and having done so much work, he still had not achieved what he needed to achieve. Then, one night, on a May full moon, he sat with strong determination (adhiṭṭhāna) under a tree, crossed his arms, crossed his legs, closed his eyes and he said, 'I will not open my eyes, my legs or arms until I finally see through and get to the end of suffering, or I die.' That is the strongest determination of all.

Now, we are unlikely to be asked to call upon such determination as this in the pursuit of our aspirations, but it is useful to reflect upon the fact that, if our aspirations are greater than our willingness to put forth the effort to fulfil them, then our aspirations are in fact rooted in both greed and entitlement. Once we come to understand the law of Dependent Origination and karma, we see for ourselves that what unfolds for us in the life is entirely the result of conditions we create or seeds sown, and the effort we make to bring these seeds to fruit. To deeply long for something and to know where to find it, but then to not find the determination to actually reach our goal, probably brings more internal suffering than not to have longed for anything at all.

Once we have understood the nature of virtue and our hearts are set in the direction of harmlessness, then our aspirations will naturally incline towards wholesome things that are for our benefit and not our detriment. Greed itself is gradually overcome and selfish desire is transformed into wholesome aspiration. Yet still we may find ourselves not progressing year by year, simply because we have not found the determination to stick at our goals and see things through to resolution.

Indolence, which is very much the attitude of, 'I can't be bothered', is a deeply depleting character trait. Nothing great is achieved without a combination of determination and humility. There are countless people who are forever coming up with good ideas, or are motivated to do something out of desire or greed, but who fail to see through to completion the things they start because of sloth and torpor and lack of determination.

Being realistic about what we are actually willing to bring to the party is a very important part of laying out our stall in life. We are all capable of great ideas, but how many of us are willing to put in the hard graft, much of which will go unnoticed and be repetitive and uninteresting, to turn a great idea into a reality? To do so takes determination.

It is important to reflect upon the relationship between aspiration and ambition and see if you can recognise where your desire to have and do things is rooted in greed, even if the things you desire in themselves may be wholesome. Then look into your level of determination or willingness to fall into indolence and let the things you have started fade away because in reality they required more determination than you could muster.

Reflect also upon the difference between the wholesome quality of determination and the unwholesome quality of wilfulness, which is simply the need to have one's own way without reflecting upon whether that is appropriate. Determination is the energy required to bring forth, through sustained effort, the things we desire. It is important that we recognise the difference between determination and wilfulness, which is simply our dogged desire and even greed for the things we want and the insistence upon having our own way.

In many ways patience and determination are the bedrock and backbone of true strength of character, and without them we are likely to be one who has many dreams, and maybe even starts many projects, but who fails to see much through to completion. Such a person makes much noise in their time but tends to produce little. It is the opposite of the person who moves quietly and unnoticed in this world but achieves great things in small understated ways.

The two qualities of patience and determination work together in support of each other, complementing each other to produce a balanced ability to put forth sustained effort.

In meditation we talk of how serenity and concentration overcome restlessness, and how energy overcomes sloth and torpor, but in life it is patience that overcomes restlessness and determination that overcomes indolence and laziness. Spend some time reflecting on these qualities and perhaps review your life for where the wholesome ones have shone through or where the hindrances have undermined you. Make an exercise of this if you have time. List the things that you have done in life that have been significant, and regardless of whether you succeeded or not, reflect upon the degree to which you found the level of determination and patience that might have been required. You can also look into your daily life and see where these two qualities might be serving you better.

## Renunciation and Restraint

Restraint and renunciation mean learning to give up what is now superfluous. Another way we haemorrhage a tremendous amount of energy is through things that actually are not that meaningful. We have become entangled and our life becomes inordinately complex because of marginal choices that actually are not really pertinent to our genuine well-being. Learning to give up the things that consume energy, that are not productive, that is what we mean by renunciation. And restraint is understanding the importance of moderation.

There are still desires to experience life in its fullness, which of course we should honour, but without restraint it is easy to consume all of our wholesome energy in the pursuit and gratification of our desires, so that little time or energy is left for the making of merit with our lives. Without restraint we quickly become overcome with greed or gluttony and our lives can easily become an unsustainable withdrawal from our deposit account.

We need both our energy and good fortune to carry us through to the end of our lives, and to not run out before we get there. Life is always about choices. Perhaps we could reflect upon the things in our lives that consume unnecessary energy and bring little by way of benefit or reward. Learning to give up what is superfluous leaves us with more energy for the things that are truly meaningful to us.

Many of the people who seek guidance from me on account of a pervasive feeling of despair in their lives, when we look even sometimes just briefly at their situation, we so often recognise that the feeling of despair is coming from not having the time to connect and develop the things that are meaningful to them. Almost always this is on account of haemorrhaging energy on things that are totally unnecessary.

## Truthfulness and Self-Honesty

Truthfulness is the next pāramī, which is a willingness to look at the terrain within which we are living and look at things honestly rather than try to package it up in a way that suits us. Self-honesty is the willingness to see things as they actually are rather than pretending that they are otherwise. And of course, this also involves honesty with regards to how we convey ourselves to others.

Even though we perhaps do not lie openly, there are many ways in which we might seek to elicit responses from others or seek their admiration by presenting ourselves in ways that are less than honest. At the end of the day, it is you yourself that you have to be with, when you are on your own, and it is you that you want to be at peace with. When you are at peace with yourself, you will much more easily be at peace with everybody else.

So this willingness to look honestly at what is going on within you is self-honesty. It is not seeking to package it up in such a way that suits you or pleases others or seeks their approval, if it is not true to yourself. This is another form of dishonesty.

Denial is an aspect of lack of self-honesty. It is not being willing to accept things as they are, and is a form of ignorance. This can severely block or disrupt the flow of awareness and its energy through our bodies. It can have a significant impact upon our health and well-being, even if at a conscious level we are using denial as a coping mechanism. Overcoming denial so that our life force can be fully expressed within us is an important part of developing our pāramī of energy. Denial plays a significant role in many forms of chronic fatigue and depression.

## Wisdom

Wisdom is insight. Our capacity for insight is another one of our pāramīs. Some people have a capacity to 'see into' quite quickly, others less so. We can see this with regard to receiving spiritual teachings. On retreat I give the teachings and explain how to practise meditation. I explain how things are, and you reflect upon these teachings. You start to see your mind changing on account of these reflections, and now you start to see life in a different way. When the wisdom faculty is strong in us, then the Dharma opens in us quite quickly and we see what needs to be done. When the wisdom faculty is poor we do not really get it. It does not cut through the position we are holding on to quite as convincingly.

Now our wisdom faculty matures with the reorganising of our mind and the disciplining and refinement of the way our mind functions, which is what our meditation practice does for us. You know, insight is always the result of our meditation. It is the fruit of our endeavour. And then, as we start to 'see into', our capacity to love becomes more unconditional, our attachments and our entitlements start to fade, and the conviction behind our other pāramīs grows.

Our capacity for wisdom, like our energy, is something that varies tremendously from person to person. It is something that we can either support by taking care of the mind, or undermine by allowing ourselves to become smothered in ignorance and inattentiveness. Once that happens, even if we had the capacity to understand, we cannot make sense of things because our mind is so poorly organised. Wisdom, like energy, indeed like all the pāramīs, is something that takes cultivation so that it can reach its potential within us.

When the Buddha realised Nibbāna[6] that night under the Bodhi tree over twenty-five centuries ago, when he freed himself from suffering and realised the culmination of his efforts, his own wisdom faculty reached its fullest potential. Having done so he made the reflection, 'That for which I came here to do, I have done.'

With this, a tremendous sense of deliverance and release came upon him as he sat, and as he was enjoying that feeling of freedom he reflected to himself, 'This Dharma that I came to see this night, this is deep and hard to understand. If I was to try to teach this to others it would be vexing both to them and to me.' And he was about to head off to the hills, to the mountains, to live a life as an ascetic of few needs and just delight in his bliss, having made the reflection, 'I'm just going to upset people if

---

6 Nibbāna is what the Buddha called 'the deathless state: that which is beyond.' For further explanation please see 'The Flavour of Liberation', Vol. 3, Chapters 24, 25 & 26.

I try and explain this to them'. And then one Brahma, whose mind was likewise bright and clear and who had been witness to the Buddha's efforts that night, saw the radiance that appeared in the Buddha's heart as he reached the cessation of suffering.

The awareness that arises in your heart produces a light, and the brilliance and colour of that light depends upon the clarity and purity of the mind. This is what we mean when we talk of the light in our hearts. And how bright it is, is a reflection of the quality of that consciousness that is arising in it. That night the Buddha's heart shone very brightly. Brahma saw this light and recognising that he was about to head off to a life of seclusion, appeared to the Buddha. Brahma said to him, 'Look, there are beings with little dust in their eyes. They will understand what you have come to see. Teach them. They will learn, they will practise and they will see what you have seen.'

And the Buddha reflected upon that, 'Ah, yes, this is true. There is a possibility.' So he made reflection, 'Who should I teach?' And he went in search of his teachers, the ones who had taught him the eight levels of absorption, or samādhi, earlier in his life. But he found that they had died while he was doing his practices alone in the forest. So he then thought, 'Well, who to teach?' And he went to see the five ascetics who had been with him when he was practising the austerities, prior to him going off alone. He thought, surely they have little dust in their eyes. He found them one month later and he taught them, and they did get it, but they did not all get it immediately. They got it gradually, some of them after receiving instructions in meditation from the Buddha.

Over the forty years that he taught, nobody got it easily, apart from the very, very few. Most of them had to put forth tremendous effort. That capacity to see is not borne of your intelligence. When we listen to Dharma we listen from the heart. Our capacity to see is actually what we call 'direct perception', and it arises within the heart, not the mind. It is in our heart, through direct perception, or direct knowledge, not through reflection, that we come to know if there is truth in the Dharma or not.

It is not whether your mind can reason it all out. Your mind can tie itself up in knots trying to think it all through. The ability to see is a reflection of the gradual maturing of this wisdom faculty and it functions at a much deeper level than intellect. And even for some of those that the Buddha taught, it was forty years of practice before they could really see through, and they had to work at it. So this wisdom pāramī is something we work on by guarding and developing the quality of our mind, so our ability to see progresses gradually.

## Loving Kindness

And then the next pāramī is loving kindness. Being kind and caring towards others. It is having regard for the welfare of others and opposes selfishness. The basic capacity for human kindness is one of the things that marks us as truly human. When we talk of that which is inhumane, we invariably are talking about attitudes that are lacking in any sense of kindness or regard for others, like cruelty.

Something very significant happens to us at a subtle energetic level when we experience the feeling of kindness or love towards another, and something equally significant happens when we experience a feeling of unkindness or incline towards another with ill-will or hatred. We talk often about the notion of being open-hearted or feeling that our heart is closed. There is more to this than just a turn of phrase. The mechanism by which we feel any kind of empathy with others and our surroundings relies upon the coherent functioning of the heart chakra and the flow of awareness through it.

When we experience such things as resentment and ill-will, it literally chokes the current of life flowing through the heart chakra, and in so doing shuts down our capacity to feel. As I have said, when we looked at the energetics behind the life experience, all of the depth of feeling that adds texture to our experience relies upon the coherent current of energy through the heart. When this current stops flowing through us, we are no longer able to feel such emotions as love.

Love is the longing for the happiness of another, what we wish for others when we reflect with kindness or empathy. This life current becomes stagnated gradually through repetitive self-centredness, anger, and ill-will. And it's because of this that we lose our ability to feel and experience love and kindness. This longing for the happiness of others is something that is strong in some and less so in others, and like our wisdom faculty, it matures or atrophies dependent upon the attitude we bring to life.

Often it requires either an act of forgiveness or generosity of spirit towards ourselves or others to allow the heart to open where it might have closed, and allow the feeling of love and kindness to be experienced more deeply within us. The more self-focused we become, the less we delight in the happiness of others. As the idea of ourselves as the centre of our world fades, we create more openness within the heart and become more able to experience love in its higher expression, or what we call unconditional love, which inclines with an attitude of kindness towards others with no expectation of anything in return.

While love is the longing for the happiness of others, compassion is the longing for the cessation of suffering of others. They are in effect two sides of the same coin, because to be happy is to be free from suffering and to suffer is to not be happy. In Pali the word for happiness is sukha and the word for suffering is dukkha (literally not-happy). Love and compassion mature equally within us as our understanding of both happiness and suffering matures.

## Equanimity

I'm often asked on retreat, 'Why is equanimity considered to be a wholesome quality of mind? Does it not mean that we do not care or that we lack interest in anything?' It could not actually be further from the truth. What they are alluding to is indolence, which may well contain in it a feeling of numbness, denial or unwillingness to be with things.

Equanimity is the quality of mind that can be completely with things as they are without rejecting them or clinging to them. It is the attitude of total acceptance. In truth it is reaching this point of total acceptance of what is, that becomes the ground for the arising of the three other truly noble qualities of mind that we call love, compassion and appreciative joy. All three of these qualities are shrunk by our either not accepting things and rejecting them with aversion, or clinging to things with attachment.

I always say to people that equanimity is the highest of all states of mind, and that it may take a very long time before we truly experience it in its highest form, and come to understand why this is the case. But even at the simplest level we can see that our mental suffering is proliferated by our inability to be with things as they are, and hugely reduced by our acceptance that it is what it is.

So these are the ten pāramīs. The development of them constitutes the development of our character in a positive way. There has been much said in recent years of the benefits of mindfulness, but in truth, while the Buddha most certainly praised the benefits of mindfulness, it is interesting that he did not include it in the list of pāramīs. Perhaps it would be helpful if we started to pay attention to a broader range of qualities within us and see what role they may play in determining whether we progress quickly or slowly, painlessly or painfully.

It is all too easy to get into a muddle in life, through making choices without thinking about them which later on impact our lives in ways that we would never have anticipated. Our life is not made better simply by packing more into it, but by our ability to engage more completely with it, which may often mean that less is more.

Our ability to engage more completely with life is hugely diminished when these pāramīs are lacking, and tremendously enriched as they develop. As I have said previously, even our ability to meditate calmly and peacefully with a clear, bright and concentrated mind will be a reflection of these pāramīs as they develop within us.

# CHAPTER FOURTEEN

# ONE LIFE

So, there are three aspects of the Buddha's teachings. The practice of meditation is at the core of the second aspect. It is important to understand that historically one would not have received instructions in the cultivation and purification of mind until becoming well established in the first aspect of the practice, which is the cultivation of right conduct, or virtue. Virtue has always historically been the bedrock of all spiritual practice and teachings. Our mind simply will not develop concentration beyond a certain point if we are not restrained in our behaviour.

The Buddha taught meditation within the context of a whole approach to life. He would not have taught meditation to anybody who had not previously made a really serious commitment to virtuous conduct, or an effort to live as harmlessly as possible.

All religions, essentially, are trying to teach us to behave appropriately and considerately. When the Buddha spoke of the time when humanity would degenerate, he did not talk of the degeneration of religion but the degeneration of the basic moral principles of behaviour, motivation and conduct that underpinned our societies. And the first branch of the Buddha's Eightfold Noble Path, the aspect of virtuous or right conduct, is teaching us to behave kindly and considerately rather than selfishly. This is something you find in all religions.

Jesus' Sermon on the Mount, one of his few direct teachings, was a teaching on virtuous conduct. It was imploring us to behave considerately. He does not tell us that to get to heaven we must go to church on a Sunday, but that the only way to improve our current condition and reach a place where we might experience the end of suffering beyond this life is through virtue.

So it is clear that faith alone is not going to carry us all the way, any more than simple understanding will. Studying the principles of swimming without ever getting in the water is no more going to keep us alive if one day we should fall overboard, than just believing we will float. Somewhere along the line we will have to learn to swim if we are going to know that we will be safe in the water.

So all religions at their heart are imploring us to behave considerately. These days, we live in a secular society in which we have tended to become somewhat cynical about religion. But the problem is, while rejecting the formulaic side of faith, we seem sadly to have also rejected the importance of putting moral conduct at the forefront of our social values. So with the decline of religion, sadly, has also come the decline in morality, and this is most unfortunate. Certainly it does not bode well if we are seeking to free ourselves from suffering.

Being the independent, free-thinking people that we are so proud of being, we do not like being told what to do, and because of this we have also rejected the essence of much of the spiritual guidance that in the past has helped to provide a moral compass by which to find our way. Of course, if we were all going to choose to behave considerately we would not need such a compass, but the jury is out as to whether we do make intelligent choices with regard to our welfare and that of those around us.

With no guidance on how to behave in recent times,  we have tended to see a degeneration of the moral values which have always been at the heart of all religious teachings. There is a danger then that we might have thrown the baby out with the bathwater on that one, just because we do not like to be told what to do.

In our insistence on personal freedom and freedom of expression, non-compliance often starts to feel like the most empowered response. We are all intelligent enough to see that we will need to consume less and learn to live simpler lives if we are going to either flourish individually or flourish as a species. While it seems we are driven almost entirely by the survival instinct these days, there is little regard for the quality of the world in which we survive. As I have said already, our technology is probably not going to kill us, but have we yet asked what it might be doing to the essence of us as humans?

The Buddha, like all great teachers of the past, implored us to behave kindly and considerately. He did not say, 'Because otherwise you are not going to get to heaven', although he did make clear that such abodes are only reached through virtue and kindness. He explained the mechanisms by which we sow the seeds for suffering, usually without knowing that we are doing it, and how we bring suffering to ourselves now and in the future on account of our behaviour and what prompts it.

So on top of pointing out a moral framework as the basis of our welfare, he taught the process by which we might train the mind in such a way that its propensity to come to suffering would be diminished. That training was the practice of meditation, through the development of both concentration and mindfulness, and through the refinement of character.

The purification of mind through meditation, or sammā-samādhi, formed the second part of the Buddha's Eightfold Noble Path. The third aspect of the Buddha's teaching is called paññā, or wisdom. This is the development of the insight that comes upon us as we learn to look more carefully, objectively and self-honestly at life. When we start to see how life really functions, we see what is called the law of Dependent Origination, or the creative intelligence behind life. We see the causal process, the creative process that we are a part of, and in seeing it our sense of entitlement is gradually dismantled and our feeling of responsibility or accountability develops.

Seeing this for ourselves is an extremely compelling experience, and when we do see for ourselves what is really going on here in life, the urge to behave selfishly is cut off at the root. Prior to that we have to learn to behave ourselves by choice and through restraint, because the tendency to be selfish or greedy or unkind may still arise in us.

The first stage is to be asked to behave nicely, which is what all religions have asked us to do. The second stage is the process of mental training by which we can start to make friends with our mind and stop fighting with it. It is the gradual training of the mind that brings it into a really coherent, organised state. From that coherent state we start to see what an extraordinary thing this life actually is. Not seeing that, is only on account of our mind being in a muddle, and the suffering we create is all on account of that confused and muddled mind.

As our mind starts to settle and become calm, we begin to see what is going on and we realise, 'Wow, OK, that's how it is'. At that point we start to restrain ourselves not just as an act of will but because we are beginning to taste the sweet fruits of having an organised mind and to recognise the misery of a messy mind.

All of the spiritual teachers of the past had our best interests at heart, because they longed for us to be free of suffering. In their different ways they had various ideas about how we might free ourselves from suffering, but all of them would agree on the fact that the first way to free yourself from suffering is to behave properly.

What marks the Buddha as profoundly different from other spiritual teachers, although not so much from the Hindu religion, is the way in which he explains the law of Dependent Origination, or the creative process, the law of cause and effect or what we call karma. Now karma does not appear on the radar of western religious thought much at all, although the Bible does indeed teach us that as we sow, so shall we reap. The effect of behaving badly according to western religious principles is that you would not be approved of by your god, or maker and may not thus be granted access to a higher state after death.

What the Buddha extremely skilfully pointed out, was the way in which we can bring the mind into a state of coherence and focused concentration whereby we can investigate the effects of our behaviour for ourselves. This process finally takes us beyond judgement of better or worse and beyond the point where we have to stand on the word of others, be they scientists or religious leaders, to the point where we start to see the intelligence behind life. He also explained how to investigate the functioning of consciousness so that we can see what happens to us as a result of our behaviour and actions.

These religious teachings have all pointed out that you do not come to a pleasurable experience at the end of this life unless you live this life in a reasonably considerate and meritorious way. The Buddha explains and teaches us how to investigate for ourselves the process by which we get there. He showed life to be an intelligent causal process, a chain of what we call dependently-arising conditions. The conditions we find within our life are the fruiting of, or the effects of, past conditions. Seeds sown in the past, fruit as conditions now.

And this is absolutely at the heart of what the Buddha was teaching us. He was teaching us how to see for ourselves that we are now experiencing the effect of past actions, and that the way that we act and behave and think and speak now will be the ground for what we experience in the future. What the Buddha taught us was that only by seeing for ourselves how things are, do we reach the point of acceptance of them as they are. This acceptance is what we call equanimity.

That is what marks the way the Buddha taught as being so different. Because our western religious teachings would have us believe that what we are experiencing is the result of a creator that decided to make it like this. What the Buddha showed us is that when you look really deeply into the law of Dependent Origination and you watch it functioning, you will see the same principle at work in absolutely everything, everywhere.

You will then understand that we are all part of a single process: one life. A single creative intelligence that does not vary from time to time, and certainly does not favour one person over another. And that you will always see, when you really look in depth, that there is not a hair out of place in this process.

Now that is an extraordinary thing to take on board. That is a very profound realisation to come to. But it is that realisation, when we come to it, that cuts off at the root all the conflict that we have with life and our place within it. When we see what is actually going on here, we sit so exquisitely and naturally in our place within it and there is no ground for conflict with it.

The path out of suffering starts with the act of acceptance that this is what it is. Because whether you understand how or why it is the way it is, it is the way it is. And the only thing you can really do if you are going to get on is to accept that it is the way it is.

Beyond that, the Buddha showed us that not only is it blatantly obvious that it is the way it is, but he showed us that it was always only ever going to be like that. And then we come to the realisation, 'Why ever did I expect it to be something different?' That puts us right bang in the centre of our own predicament, right in the driving seat, utterly accountable and responsible for ourselves, and that is a very empowering place to be.

As the Buddha said to those around him just before he died, 'Decay is inherent in all compound things. Work out your own salvation with diligence.' What he was basically saying was, 'Look, I may have shown you the way, but I have not saved anyone. I have not worked anybody's way out of suffering.'

Each and every single one of us has to free ourselves from suffering, and no-one else is going to do that for us. Though someone may come along and give us a helping hand from time to time, nobody else is going to take away from us our own tendency to bring ourselves to grief but us. And that is what the Buddha said. He told us that he, the Buddha, has not saved anyone, nobody has ever saved anyone else and that we must work it out for ourselves.

So what he was doing was showing us how to take responsibility for ourselves. The path that he taught was the process by which we take that responsibility, and as such meditation is only a part.

This word Dharma is used in Sanskrit, and in Pali the word is Dhamma. One of the meanings of it is truth. It is an extraordinarily loaded word. But what it means is the way of things, the suchness of it. The Buddha was teaching us the way of things. He was asking us to look directly into the nature of our experience, unclouded by views or expectations. Once we have come to see things as they are, this becomes our teacher.

It is the understanding of what is suffering which is the first Noble Truth. The understanding of the cause of suffering is the second Noble Truth. The understanding of what is the cessation of suffering is the third Noble Truth, and the way, or the path, that leads to the cessation of suffering is the fourth Noble Truth. This is what the Buddha was asking us to see for ourselves.

That effectively is what the Buddha taught, but it is also what we come to see. And it is when we see it that it becomes a living Dharma. As I stated at the very beginning of the book, the Dharma is nothing more than a living principle that we are all experiencing. It is not just a doctrine that we read on the page or hear expounded by a teacher. It is the very process of life that we are living. The Dharma points directly at life and the principles by which it functions, manifests, works and behaves, which we too are a part of. It is a living and dynamic principle, and meditation is a way to look deeply enough into it to stop being confused or surprised by what is going on.

Overcoming our confusion is surely a worthwhile achievement. But the Buddha is not suggesting we solve our confusion by having a jolly good think about life. He is asking us to learn to pay attention. If you had spent an hour meditating for every hour you spent trying to figure out what on earth this is all about, you may well have got there by now. You would probably have come to see for yourself, without standing or leaning upon the word of others which is something else the Buddha told us to be careful of. He said, 'Do not believe what I say because people call me the Buddha, learn to look and see for yourselves.'

So what do we see when we glimpse beyond the veil of appearances to the truth that lies behind them? We see that what we might have assumed to be the roots of suffering, things like greed, selfishness, anger and hatred, are not innate within any being. These things are all the result of confusion. It is ignorance, or not understanding, that is the real cause of our suffering.

Any being who is not confused about what is going on here will experience the fading away, in stages, of greed, selfishness, anger and hatred. It is the very seeing of what you are a part of that performs the function of cutting off those things. So if you think that it is greed and hatred, selfishness and all the other things that is the root of suffering, it is not. Confusion, not understanding, ignorance is the cause of suffering.

Ignorance is resolved by coming to know, by coming to see for yourself. So this exercise of meditation, if you really see it for what it is, is a little bit more than an exercise in how to manage your stress or concentrate upon your breath. It is a doorway through to an understanding of life and your part in it. And at many levels it is probably what we came here for; to figure this all out for ourselves so we can make our peace with it?

As the Buddha said, there is a way that leads to certainty, to clarity, beyond doubt. That place of being beyond doubt is the place of seclusion and peace and the end of suffering. We are only afraid, we are only full of doubt because we are confused. We do not know. But the extraordinary and wonderful thing is that when you do see for yourselves, what you see is awesome.

We only made a right old muddle of it because we did not understand what was going on. It is a great shame really, and one over which many tears have been shed. I suppose if we had been given a proper user's manual when we arrived here, a proper set of instructions, we might not have made such a muddle of it.

But the encouraging thing is that of all those who have walked the path to the point of seeing for themselves, none of them have come back and said, 'Oh dear, what a frightful place this is.' They have all come back convinced that it is truly amazing. It is in their inability to express just how amazing it is that it comes to be called divine.

It was not that the Buddha failed to recognise this extraordinary process, but that he recognised how, in our confusion, we are at great risk of causing so much suffering for ourselves and others. But when you see it, when you see the extraordinary intelligence at work in all of this, your willingness to harm yourself in the pursuit of what you want will end.

The stillness that I ask you to connect to when you start your meditation has more intelligence in it than you have even begun to understand. Behind the arising and passing of things and their display, behind our entanglement with it, our true nature rests effortlessly within itself, in a state of stillness and peace that has never been disturbed, and it has never been in conflict.

When we stop for a moment and really look out at the world, not the one we as humans have created, but the one that is expressing itself everywhere as nature, we do not see that it is in conflict, but that it rests effortlessly within itself, as it has done for countless ages. It has maintained itself, kept itself in balance, tidied itself up on its own and maintained the life that flows through it effortlessly. The world is not inherently in conflict. The only thing in conflict is our idea of ourselves as humans, each of us individually and as a group. And it is the letting go, in stages, of our intoxication and fixation with the idea of ourself that puts us gradually back in touch with that intelligence that really governs life. And that process is the process of coming gradually out of suffering.

So in your insistence on having your own way and not liking to be told what to do, and all the freedoms you seek to grant for yourself, before you insist on them, ask yourself whether you yet know better. It is not your personal freedom, and securing it, that marks the end of your suffering. It is your willingness to live in accordance with the principles and intelligence that is actually governing life. Coming into alignment with that and not being in conflict with it is the only path out of suffering there has ever been. The Buddha did not create this path, he simply pointed it out, in case we could not see it for ourselves.

# CHAPTER FIFTEEN

# AWAKENING IN AN AGE OF DEGENERATION

## Chatral Rinpoche: A Prayer in a Time of Ecological Crisis

*Buddhas and bodhisattvas of the ten directions,*
*Turn your enlightened intention towards us!*
*May all sentient beings tormented by this present age*
*Of the five virulent degenerations,*
*Know that they possess a treasure that can alleviate*
*The various portents of decay in the physical world and its inhabitants*
*Due to the ripening of their wrong intentions and actions.*

*A treasure grounded in the renunciation of harmful actions*
*And the cultivation of altruistic actions,*
*Granting all the spiritual and temporal well-being one could desire.*
*This is the supreme wish-fulfilling gem of good heart*
*Associated with all supreme spiritual practices.*

*Endowed with this (good heart),*
*May all beings cultivate love and compassion for one another,*
*Without hatred, and without fighting or quarrelling.*
*May they enjoy the glorious resources of happiness -*
*All they could possibly desire,*
*And swiftly attain the level of conclusive awakening!*

Over twenty-five centuries ago, the Buddha spoke of an age of degeneration when beings lose their moral compass and become obsessed solely with selfish pursuits at great detriment to themselves, others and the world in which they live. Below is a list of the five signs of degeneration that he identified.

# The Five Virulent Degenerations:

**1. The Degeneration of Time.** The quality of things deteriorates, food becomes less nutritious, grain tastes less good and does not ripen, the environment becomes degraded, famine and wars proliferate, and new diseases arise.

**2. The Degeneration of Disturbing Emotions**. The virtue of householders declines, negative emotions proliferate, ideas of self proliferate to the point where pride, competitiveness and greed become so embedded that beings find it almost impossible to surmount them.

**3. The Degeneration of Views**. Wrong view proliferates, beings cannot see what is happening to them and reject the truth when it is spoken. They tend to believe in wrong philosophies and find it hard to believe in right view. They reject the law of karma and Dependent Origination. The majority hold views that are morally degenerate, and become intolerant to the point of hatred.

**4. The Degeneration of Physical Form**. Appearance degenerates, obesity proliferates, intellect degenerates, good health degenerates, beings become harder to help and harder to subdue.

**5. The Degeneration of the Life Span**. Afflictive conditions proliferate and gradually the life span shortens.

At times such as these the choices that beings make will determine their welfare or suffering. Of these five signs which the Buddha described that mark the coming of an age of degeneration, one of them is that beings reject the truth even when it is put in front of them. The truth, in the end, is right in front of us every day if we are only willing to see it. The question is — are we willing to pay attention?

There are many reasons put forth for the demise of organised religion in societies that have gone through development into the modern world order. Religion is often seen now as a violation of personal freedom. We have fought as many wars over our rights to freedom of choice as we have over religion, but freedom of choice only ever leads to flourishing in the hands of those who make intelligent and virtuous choices. In the hands of those who do not, it quickly leads to degeneration.

It is not just religion that we have rejected in our modern world. We have removed a sense of the sacred from almost everything in our lives. Marriage is not sacred, bearing children is not sacred, sex is not sacred, our planet is not sacred, we do not view each other as sacred. Recently there has been a tremendous effort put forth to bring meditation to the masses in the form of mindfulness, in the hope that it might ease the stresses and strains we are experiencing in trying to make sense of our position in a modern world. In doing so, almost all of the spiritual context within which it was originally taught has been removed, in the hope that it might not offend or put anyone off or be seen in any way as some kind of indoctrination.

I was approached a while ago and asked to put together an eight week course in meditation, the brief being that I had to make sure that all spiritual references or references to the source of the teachings were removed, so that it could be taught in schools and hospitals. I was effectively asked to remove the spiritual context from the teachings, which have historically helped us to find just that within our lives.

Have we ever stopped to ask whether it might be the case that the alarming increase in depression and hopelessness that so many otherwise fortunate human beings are now experiencing, might actually be because they lack that very spiritual context in their lives? While we may initially think what we need are tools by which to cope better with life as it is, at a deeper level I believe we are actually longing to find a deeper sense of meaning while questioning the actual direction we are heading. That is what so many of us today are actually looking for. What we are being offered are tools by which we can cope well enough to stay on the trajectory we are on. However it is not help to stay on course that we need, but encouragement to embrace a wholesale change.

I have little doubt that there are countless people out there just waiting for permission to embrace a quantum change of direction. Experience suggests that deep and profound change tends only to happen when it is thrust upon us. The problem with this, is that forced change inevitably brings with it far more suffering and hardship than the choices we make for ourselves consciously. A slap in the face with a wet fish, though unpleasant, is not nearly as difficult to live with as being knocked off your feet and the ground giving way beneath you: but if it serves to wake us up before we fall asleep at the wheel, it has served an important purpose. The further out of alignment with the truth behind our lives we get, the more inconvenient that truth feels.

Meditation is the pathway by which we gradually come to reject the things that are for our detriment and delight in the things that are for our genuine welfare. It helps us reach a point of willingness to let go rather than begrudge the idea of having to do so. If we begrudge the suggestion that we need to change, it is usually not just because it is inconvenient, but because it interferes with our personal ambitions and the pursuit of our goals and desires. Meditation helps us gradually bring into focus the things that are actually meaningful in our lives and the things that are causing us suffering.

When I left my last teacher in Sikkim, at the end of years of intensive training in meditation, his final request to me was to return home and to continue to meditate for the benefit of others. Over the years, many people have come on retreat with me to learn meditation, and almost all of them come hoping that meditation will in some way enrich their lives.

At the end of retreat, I explain to them the two basic principles that our welfare and progress in the future stand upon. Firstly, if we are going to continue to centre our life around the pursuit of our desires, we will need to be totally unwilling to harm others or ourselves in the pursuit of our desires. The second is that if we wish to secure our welfare for the future, we should not expect to take out more than we put in.

These principles are in effect nothing more than expressions of the basic principles that govern all life. It is living in alignment with the intelligence behind life that brings flourishing and happiness, and living in conflict that brings degeneration, despair and suffering.

So let us return to the four kinds of beings and the direction in which we are heading.

Those born in the light and moving into the light are those rare individuals who recognise their good fortune as most certainly not to be taken for granted. They have turned their supporting karma towards improving the welfare of others, and in doing so give more than they take out in life. They are maintaining their good fortune for the future.

Those born in the light and moving into the darkness are those beings who, intoxicated with the pursuit of their desires and turning their accumulation of past merit solely to the gratification of those desires, are taking out far more than they put in. These are the group who are spending their investment account in an unsustainable way, and in doing so causing suffering both for those around them and for themselves, now and in the future.

Those born in the darkness moving into the light are those unfortunate individuals who struggle to find support for their lives, and yet in spite of this, surmount the tendency to feel hard done by and instead turn their lives to the patient improving of their lot, by giving of themselves in some way that improves their welfare and the welfare of others.

Those born in the darkness and moving into the darkness are those unfortunate individuals who, finding themselves in a position of hardship, fail to find the humility to accept that their life is as it is, and expect it to improve without making the efforts for it to do so. And beyond that even seeking to take from others what they have rightfully acquired, rather than seeking or accepting the generosity of others for support.

This is how we might reflect upon the second principle for our welfare, namely overcoming the confused belief that it is appropriate to take out more than we put in.

The planet that we have lived upon has managed itself for billions of years, sustaining a balance whereby the life that it sustained did not draw out more than it put in. Life has been perfectly recycled at every level without any accumulation of toxic waste or any diminishing of the natural resources that support it. The oceans and rivers remained pure and teemed with life, the oxygen cycle and the nitrogen cycle were kept perfectly in balance, and everything that died decayed without leaving any toxic residue from its presence here. And all of this occurring naturally without anyone managing it or interfering with it in any way.

This basic principle of life governs the fortune or abundance that we experience in life and the ease with which we are supported. It has taken a tremendous amount of resource for us to be born and grow to maturity so that we can embark upon this adventure of life with any hope of finding joy and fulfilment in it. Even the decision to bring forth life by bearing children needs to be made after reflecting on whether or not we have the requisites by which to support that life we intend to bring forth. When we do this without making such a reflection, we put in place a renewed cycle of suffering. Being born without the support we need for our lives is a reflection of a lack of good fortune.

One of the ways we accumulate such good fortune is by providing for those who come after us in some way, whether it be as parents or as contributors to the welfare of our communities and societies. When we fail to find ways to contribute, we start the transition out of good fortune into misfortune, or from misfortune to continued misfortune and suffering. Whether we are relying upon our investment account or running on overdraft in our life, once we draw more than we deposit, it is only a matter of time before we can no longer take for granted the support for life we have grown used to.

This fundamental principle governs life at absolutely every level, and it is utterly non-judgmental, not favouring one being over another.

Most of the despair that exists in the world today is on account of us not getting the things we want, whether that is the rice and water needed to feed our children or the promotion we are hoping for at work. When we stop seeing our good fortune as a rare and extraordinary blessing and start to take it for granted, we start the gradual and inexorable process of the degeneration of our consciousness and bring to an end the time of our flourishing on this planet.

We may well not have much materially to give, but we may be one of those fortunate few who are not spending their entire time struggling just to uphold their elaborate lives. Sometimes the signs of good fortune may not be what they appear, and we may not always recognise the opportunities that come our way. It is a sign of degeneration of consciousness when those of good fortune suffer more than those with little.

When I lived in Bali, I lived by the sea in a quiet fishing community. One day I was standing on the beach with a local fisherman who was fishing. An American tourist walked past and started talking with us. The man fishing pulled in his line and took two small fish off the hooks. Placing them in a bucket beside him he started packing up to leave.

'Hey, pal! Why don't you trail three lines at a time? That way you would catch more fish. That way you could get what you need for your family and sell the rest at the market. If you then saved up one day you could buy a boat and trail a whole bunch of lines and catch a whole bunch of fish. I bet it wouldn't take long before you could hire someone else to go fishing for you and then you would be free to do anything you want.'

'But I am doing what I want,' said the fisherman with a smile, as he turned and walked off up the beach.

The Buddha suggested that it is through the relinquishing of our greed and need for more, that we free ourselves from suffering. He came to this conclusion because he saw such a pervasive tendency for beings to bring misery upon themselves in the pursuit of what they want. There are, however, hosts of beings who have upheld their virtue and continue to experience the wondrous display of life from a position of relative ease.

The devas in the heavenly realms are also experiencing their domain with a similar or even greater sense of ease. Such beings object to the Buddha's conclusion that life is suffering because they do not currently experience it as such, quite rightly making the reflection, 'Wait a minute. This life and our world are so very extraordinary and wonderful, surely it would be a travesty if we did not delight in it and enjoy it in all its splendour.'

They are right, of course. But the truth is that the only beings who genuinely do come to delight in life and all its splendour are those who have a limit to what they are willing to do in the pursuit of their desires, which is why harmlessness is the other basic principle for the welfare of beings.

Let's say there was something you wanted very badly. What would you be willing to do to get it, if you were willing to harm yourself or others in the pursuit of your desires? If you wanted it badly enough, perhaps there would be no end to which you would not go to acquire it. This is the point at which life begins to degenerate. Only when we are unwilling to cause suffering to ourselves and others in the pursuit of our desires does that pursuit not lead to our demise. There are countless examples today where the acquiring of the things we want brings intense suffering to others, and yet we still find ways to sanction it. This breakdown of moral conscience is the second sign of what the Buddha called the virulent degeneration of consciousness.

All of this is an expression of the total failure to reflect upon the sacred nature of life itself, as well as an expression of a willingness to cause suffering to others in the pursuit of what we want. There are countless examples where we take out more than we contribute and are willing to cause suffering both to ourselves and others by doing so. No one is telling us what we should and should not do. As fortunate human beings we are free to choose for ourselves, but we do need to understand that the choices we make define not just our present, but our future.

The Buddha said that times of virtuous governance were a reflection of the virtue of the people. Times of corrupt or unvirtuous governance are a reflection of their lack of virtue. We flourish, be it under the guidance of others or when left to make decisions for ourselves, only when we ourselves choose to uphold a basic moral code that would stop short of allowing us to cause harm or suffering to another.

So there are five things that are recommended for the welfare of householders like us who are wishing to make progress in our lives and limit the degree of hardship and suffering we experience. Those five guidelines on conduct are:

**1. To not take life**, and if you can, to try to not harm another being deliberately.

2. **To not take what is not yours.**

**3. To not speak falsely**, and if you can, to not speak in such a way that would bring people to opinions that would be to the detriment of another, i.e. to not gossip or slander or talk harshly. To not lie but to be honest, and above all to be honest with yourself.

**4. To not engage in sexual misconduct**, which is such activity that is a scattering of your energy and spirit in a way that brings suffering to yourself and others, or the breaking of promises or vows to a partner, or the causing of another to break such promises. And beyond this to show moderation with regard to lust, because lust is a deep, deep instinctual drive and it takes tremendous strength of character to not be driven by it. Much of the suffering in this world is not caused by what it may at first appear to be. Far more of it than we might think is on account of not being able to restrain our lust.

5. **To not intoxicate yourself to the point of losing your mindfulness** where you might behave in ways that you never normally would.

These five commitments to conduct, or as they are called in Pali, sīla, are the guidelines for the protection of our basic welfare. In truth, to think we are going to make progress in meditation without being willing to do our best with regard to these five things is just vanity.

So it is important to reflect upon the degree to which you feel you could make an aspiration to keep those five precepts. These five precepts, or commitments, are for our protection from coming to grief or unnecessary suffering in ways that we might not be able to anticipate. So many times we see people whose lives have been completely undone by moments of negligence or decisions that were made while their mind was driven by anger, greed, lust or pride.

One of my teachers was a famous healer in Burma. He was the last in a long line of traditional medicine men, and I spent many years working with him and learning how to make and administer his medicines. The medicines themselves were wonderful indeed, and over the years I have seen some wonderful results in those who used them.

Although I would not ask my students to do the same, every time he offered the medicine to anyone he would tell them that for as long as they wished to take it, they must uphold the five commitments. One day I asked him if it was an absolute requirement that people taking the medicine would keep their precepts, to which he replied, 'The medicine is merely for relieving the afflictions of the body. The precepts are what frees them from suffering. That is how they really heal themselves.'

He was right in so many ways. It is our conduct that is our greatest protection. To seek to be free of suffering without understanding that doing so will require us to live virtuously and considerately is, as I have said, little more than vanity.

# CHAPTER SIXTEEN

# THREE PATHS OUT OF SUFFERING

**M**editation might not be for everybody but it does help us reach a certain place of understanding and realisation that is helpful to us. It is therefore important to reflect on what other ways there might be to achieve this.

In some ways meditation might be for those really stubborn folk who will not let go until they absolutely know what they are going to get. Of course, there is little faith in such an approach.

The point is, you are never going to know what you are going to get when you let go the ego and its clinging to self, until you let go. There is no insight that is going to utterly convince you. You are a bit stuck if you are going to stand on insight alone. Sooner or later you have to let go, and you are not ever really going to know what comes next until you do. So faith or trust, sooner or later, will have to play a part in your journey. Wisdom alone will not free you.

In the same way that the Buddha said we need to balance serenity with energy so as not to fall into over or under-exertion, so too we need to balance faith and wisdom. He did not say we need a lot of wisdom and a little faith, or a lot of faith and a little wisdom. He said we needed both in equal measure. He said this so many times and yet (as is typical of our intellectual approach to almost everything now), we have chosen, with regard to the Dharma, to come down in favour of trying to develop insight, while not making much effort to overcome our unwillingness to find faith.

The fact that we feel the need to dilute these teachings, which for centuries have served countless beings in freeing themselves from suffering, the fact that before allowing them to make their way into mainstream consciousness we feel we need to prove their effectiveness scientifically, is a sign of our lack of faith. The problem is that the bit that we can quantifiably and scientifically verify in no way represents the pith or essence of the path and practice. The real transformation that brings us out of suffering most often goes on at a level that we may not fully understand even when it has happened to us.

It is a shame that we have taken mindfulness in isolation in our search for a spiritual solution to the problem of the increasing sense of despondency and depression that we see in our modern societies. Taking what is only the most preliminary approach to it, we seem to have put forward the idea that mindfulness practice is the essence of what the Buddha was teaching us.

As I have already said, mindfulness itself is not in the Buddha's list of pāramīs, or qualities of character to be developed by one who hoped for swift and painless progress upon the path out of suffering. Perhaps this is because mindfulness itself is morally neutral and could be taken in isolation from the rest of the Dharma, avoiding the necessity to frame it within the wider context of the Buddha's teachings.

But what if the same efforts and resources had been put into studying the helpful benefits of any of the other aspects of training; be it virtue, generosity, patience, determination or energy, for example. Perhaps if we had been encouraged as vocally to practise and develop virtue or loving kindness in our schools and workplaces, we may have felt that we were being preached to. Perhaps it is because we are able to start to develop mindfulness without having to make any concessions or give up any of the things that might be at the root of our suffering.

It is true that mindfulness was indeed highly encouraged by the Buddha, but so too were concentration and harmlessness, discipline and moral conduct. The practice of mindfulness does not ask us to make many concessions with regard to the pursuit of our desires and this is probably why we are willing to accept it as a new panacea to our modern predicament. In fact, far from being taught as a catalyst for deep-rooted change, mindfulness is rather taught as a way to cope better with the life we are leading, rather than question whether or not that life is ultimately for our well-being. Sooner or later we may have to acknowledge that the most effective of medicines are rarely sweet tasting.

For years I have tried to teach western laypeople the path of Dharma through the development of insight, but sooner or later we have to understand that it is not our mind that is going to experience freedom. The freedom we experience, when it comes upon us, is the freedom from our mind. The problem is, because we cannot see what we might be left with when we do let go our idea of ourself, we find it inordinately difficult to let go, even when the evidence in favour of it is extremely compelling.

So the path that I am teaching is what might traditionally have been called Raja Yoga. It is the yoga by which one reaches a state of union through the cultivation of one's mind. Through the practice of concentration and the refinement of character, we eventually reach an experience that is beyond self, and that experience itself puts us in front of something so complete that it dismantles the remaining aspects of ego for us, in stages.

But of course many people still fall short, in spite of all their efforts, because even when they have removed almost all of the obstacles, they still fail to glimpse what might remain. They are still trying to anticipate what the experience might be in their mind, so they still hold on because they are not sure yet. Such a person gets stuck half way, not on account of lack of insight and understanding, but because of a lack of faith.

You have done all that work to try to understand, and it is almost understood, but you are not going to get the last bit of the jigsaw that is going to finally convince you to let go, until you do let go. Because it is in the letting go that you get the last piece of the jigsaw. It is the ultimate Catch-22. Sooner or later, no matter how far you go to try to convince yourself, you are always going to come to a point that requires an act of faith.

In contrast to this approach where wisdom leads the way and faith follows, there is another way. This is the path of devotion, where faith blazes the trail and our insight emerges in stages on the back of that. The path of devotion involves putting your heart towards something that you do not understand fully but that you feel moved by, even if it starts out as just an idea.

It is a path that starts when something in your heart recognises the possibility of something sublime and taintless and beyond suffering, and you just open your heart to the idea of it and you get close to it simply by opening to it. This is what we mean by surrender. This is the path of devotion to the sacred, or what is called Bhakti Yoga. There comes a point with all of my students where I introduce them to this as an integral part of the path.

One of the key points I am making throughout this book is that so many people feel life to be so dry these days and the reason we have become so intoxicated with the pursuit of pleasure, is because we have started to lose the feeling of being connected to something sacred. Life itself is all too often reduced to its constituent parts, broken down and analysed, and then seen as nothing more than an expression of materiality becoming conscious. And it is often not seen as sacred, let alone divine. And this is one of the reasons we are so willing to disrespect life in the pursuit of what we want.

Of course, for the path of devotion to point the way out of suffering, we have to have the discernment to open our heart in the right direction, and this is where insight plays its part. We have to be willing to make sufficient reflection to see that what we are doing might be for our welfare and not our detriment. But once we do open our heart, we might often find we arrive at our goal even before we get all the pieces of the jigsaw.

That is what faith is, it is trust. It is a willingness to let go in spite of the fact that you have not fully understood yet. It gets you to a point beyond yourself even though you did not know where that would land you. The path of devotion understands that we do not even understand until we have let go. So that is another way that we can get beyond ourselves to an experience that is free of suffering.

I am teaching most people through the insight route, because we have so little faith. Nobody believes anything anymore, they are just not willing to. So I try really hard to point the path out to you in such a way that you are convinced enough by your own reflection. But in your needing to be convinced, your need to be convinced is still in your way. In your need to be convinced, you do not let go until you are convinced, and that may leave you sitting on the fence a lot longer than you have to.

So the other way, which is what I teach on retreat from time to time, when the students have reached a point of receptivity and clarity of mind, is to simply show, to point out the experience through transmission, to give the student a direct experience for themselves, and leave folk to make their own sense of it. But you have to be receptive to the experience to receive the transmission, and that takes an open heart.

So when the mind is strong in insight but weak in faith, when the mind is still waiting to understand completely before it will let go its grip - the heart does not open enough to the experience, to the point where it is fully moved, and fully knows what has happened, even when the transmission is given. Without faith you have to walk all the way to the end of the path and hope that then you will be convinced enough to let go.

The Buddha used to say that those whose insight is excessive and faith lacking tend towards cunning and believe that they can work it all out for themselves and make up their own way to suit them. To such people he pointed out that the mind will always seek to attach to views that uphold its position and reject the ones that challenge it. The path to awakening requires humility to acknowledge that we do not know it all and that it is OK. That is the point at which faith can start to carry us forward.

The third way to approach the path is through service, or Karma Yoga. We get beyond the ego, get beyond ourselves through service to others, and slowly, through the doing of things for others, one's personal sense of needs fades, and one reaches a state of selflessness, and in that way one finds grace. One comes to the experience of unification through the heart opening that is borne of service.

People often ask me why do I teach such a fortunate group of humans? Well it is partly because that is the group in front of me, but also I choose to teach such a group of people because I believe and hope that being so fortunate, they might be able to make a difference to those around them, when they do get beyond their needs and realise they have so much to offer to others.

Most of those I teach are strong in intellect. They do not struggle to understand the principles behind the Dharma, yet they are still not free from suffering. It is because they do not have enough faith and have not embraced service into their lives sufficiently to overcome the hindrances that still need to be overcome. Many of the pāramīs are more swiftly developed through service and devotion than through meditation and study. So service is the third path or way that we might dismantle the ego and open to the experience that is beyond sense of self.

I dare say if we spend as much time doing things for others as we spend worrying what others think of us, or whether we are seen the way we want to be seen, we may well be quite close to home by now. But as they say, vanity has got the better of us, and this is something that service and devotion helps us to overcome.

But whichever way it is — whether it is insight and the cultivation of your mind, or whether it is through devotion and the opening of your heart, or whether it is through service and the reaching of a state of humility and grace — all of these require you to surrender at some point your need to feel in control of your world and your need to be seen.

Now on another level it could be argued that we are not the most fortunate people in the world, not if our perceived need to understand is so great that there is almost no faith, or if our personal needs are so great that we do not feel able to do things for others. Anybody, at any time, regardless of their position or predicament, could find grace, could surrender to what is in front of them and accept that that is how it is, and open up, and in doing so see something that lies beyond that, which would free them.

Remember this when you are putting the pieces of the jigsaw together, trying to figure it out. Remember this when you are trying to decide for yourself whether it is OK to let go, whether it will be alright. When you are struggling with your unwillingness to let go, try to mix a little faith with that sharp, intelligent mind of yours. Find some trust. Because it is that faith that we have almost reasoned out of existence. And it is in this way that we make our world a dry and barren place to be. That is the nature of faith, is it not? It would not be faith if you knew what you were going to get.

In truth, this life is far more extraordinary than you think it is and you are not going to figure it out by sitting there thinking about it, or looking at it under a microscope. Folk have been doing that since the beginning of time. You do not learn by bending it to your will and insisting that you get your way. Let's stop putting terms on it. See what role just opening your heart to it and trusting it will play in freeing you from the bondage that you feel entangled with.

We must have over 1,000 hours of discourses, plus a manual on the mechanics of meditation, mental training and the progression of insight in three volumes, but none of those discourses equate to seeing, coming to know, being touched in the same way that sitting with the teacher and coming to our own direct experience touches us. It is the experience we need, not just the understanding.

But it is alright to let go. When I look out there, when I tune into it, it feels almost as if the world is holding its breath, desperately hoping, waiting, for all of us to let go. It feels as though it is waiting for us to get over ourselves. To get over the idea that we are the creators. To get over our intoxication with the idea of ourselves as the creator, so we can start to recognise the creative process that we are a part of.

Please, when you are meditating, meditate from your heart and not your head. And stop trying to figure it all out. If you really meditate from your heart and allow things to be what they are, one day you will see there is no need to figure it out.

So at this point I am going to stop feeding you insight. You have had enough, I have explained enough, I am not going to explain the last little bits to try and convince you that it is worth doing. Your heart, something in your heart, already knows that it is worth doing. So maybe you should start listening to it.

Ask your heart if what you think your needs are, really are your needs. See what you actually could give up, let go or share with others and still be fine, even better than you are now, far better.

Then you might start asking what you can do for others with all that extraordinary good fortune, and in doing so there might a chance that with this life you renew the merit that you came in here with. And that would be a very fine thing.

Over the years we have had upwards of three thousand people come on these retreats to learn meditation and insight. I see how much their lives have improved and how much healing has gone on but I am not so sure how much real letting go there has been. So what does it take? It takes more than your meditation and mindfulness practice. It takes a commitment to your virtue and it takes an act of faith.

When I ask you to tune in to the stillness of the room, do you not think perhaps that there might be something a little more in that stillness than you have yet imagined?

Jesus called it 'the peace that passes all understanding.' The Buddha was so moved by it that he devoted the remaining forty-five years of his life to teaching others the way to it. It most certainly is not just the stillness of the room, or the forest, or whatever, that we touch when we let go.

Whatever you personally choose to call it, when you touch it for yourselves you will know you have touched it and you will not need me to convince you anymore. That is when you will understand that in that equanimity, in that stillness, is the highest experience of love that you will ever, ever experience. That is when you will understand that this world and everything in it is not just appearing randomly out of emptiness, but that the basis for it all is love, and if it fails to express itself as that, it is only on account of what we have put in the way.

# CHAPTER SEVENTEEN

# THE BOUNDLESS POWER OF LIFE

Have a look outside, or even better, go outside. Why do you think I have asked you to come out here? Hopefully it is a beautiful day with a clear blue sky. Yes, the sky. That vast, cloudless expanse of clear blue sky. Take it in. Because that is what the real essence of your mind is, exactly like that, endless, cloudless, spacious clarity. There is a clear light that appears when our mind comes to cessation and our awareness remains, and it is as clear and spacious and expansive as an endless blue sky, and as luminous as the sun without being in the slightest bit blinding. It is transparent, not opaque and clouded, and it is pure luminosity. On a cloudless day, the sky is like awareness itself.

Go out on a cloudless day and gaze into the sky and immerse yourself in the expansive, spacious clarity of it, because that is the closest thing you will find to how your mind becomes when it is empty. It is not a barren, vacuous space of ignorance and blankness, it is pure and mirror-like, and whatever stillness you have ever beheld, it is stiller by far than that.

So go out into nature on a clear, bright day and try to tune in to the stillness behind the movement of things. Rest in the stillness behind the arising and passing of the sounds, the birds flying by and everything else. Rest undisturbed by what arises and passes within it. Try for yourself when you are next in nature to tune into it and get a sense of how everything is resting effortlessly within itself. As you look out there at nature, try to get the sense of how that which does appear within the vast expanse of awareness itself, has a natural tendency to rest effortlessly within itself. There is no friction in that coming into being and passing away.

So take that to your heart. Take an impression of it deep into your heart and reflect upon what I mean when I say to you, 'Rest effortlessly within yourself. Leave everything as it is.' And see if you can feel what it does to your heart when you turn up and tune in like that. I am not asking you what it does to your mind, I am asking you to leave your mind empty and just tune in to it as it is, taking nothing, adding nothing to the moment, but just resting in it.

There is nothing to be added. What the Buddha was pointing at was not a complex world view for us to subscribe to or reject, but an experience that he hoped each of us in time would come to have for ourselves. It was an experience which freed him from suffering, not a view. And it is an experience that frees all of us in time. And that is the experience of the vast, spacious clarity of the awareness that remains when our mind fades away, and it is the experience of innate stillness that rests behind the coming and going of things, that is the very basis for their arising. If you could read between the lines and glimpse the essence of what the Buddha is teaching us, that is what he is pointing to.

So here is a question for you. If emptiness is the ground of all things, and if it really is just emptiness, why do you suppose ice crystals are so beautiful? Why is everything in nature so beautiful?

They are not just unique each time they appear, they are beautiful. Why would they express themselves so beautifully, so effortlessly? Why does nature express itself so beautifully and so effortlessly? How did it manage to do such a thing for billions of years before our arrival here? On a beautiful day like this, when nature is in order and the elements are balanced, there is a conscious living intelligence that is very close to us that is extremely sublime, that rests in the background. And it is never not there.

Well, nature everywhere forms ordered and beautiful structures, and it is not just awareness that rests in the background supporting this vast array of life. Awareness itself does not create anything. Dependent Origination is the creative principle, and volition is the cause for the coming into being. Why then does nature express itself so beautifully? Why do snow crystals express themselves so beautifully? Why, do you suppose that they are not just arbitrary frozen lumps as they would be if you just exposed them to an ordinary state of mind?

The Buddha does not teach this explicitly, he merely hints at it. But if you do one day really touch that stillness that rests in the background, you will find there is something there, also resting in the background, that holds all of this endlessly. And it is pure, and it is boundless, and it is love, and this planet in its absence would be a barren place.

We have become so intoxicated with the idea of ourselves as the creator that we have lost our connection to the creative process itself. Well I am going to tell you a little story about why I left my monastery. One day, one beautiful day, when the air was still crisp and the ground was dewy, I got up very early from my bed to meditate. I cast my mind out across the forest and everything was still at rest, and I realised it was more peaceful at that time than at any other time.

I had been practising samādhi for many months, and yet there was a stillness present in that morning that was beyond anything that my mind entered into through its own efforts. Although sublimely peaceful, it was never endlessly so, in the way that everything around me felt to be that morning. And I sat and meditated and entered into a state of samādhi that was so unlike anything I had experienced before. It was no creation of my own mind as the jhānas I had been practising were, it was simply a spontaneously present state that sustained itself, that rested effortlessly within itself.

After some time, I found myself looking down upon what I thought at first was a great temple. I was so amazed by it. I moved closer with my mind to observe it and I realised that it was the head piece of an extraordinary being, so vast that I was terrified, deeply terrified just to behold it. I experienced an awe that I cannot begin to describe, and I could not bring myself to behold it for more than a moment. I moved away, what felt like far away, so that I could see without being terrified, and that was all that I could do, just witness it. This being sat in a state of samādhi so unfathomably deep and profound that the state that I was in paled into nothing and I thought I was just going to expire or be absorbed completely into it. And in the moment that I was touched by that consciousness, I knew that it was everywhere. And I knew that it was love, the purest kind of love imaginable.

One thing I knew, I knew absolutely in that moment, was that the quality of this being's mind was something that so far surpassed anything I could previously even have imagined or contemplated. I knew in that moment that it is everywhere, all the time, and it is endless, boundless love. It is love that is the intelligence that supports life. It is not an active intelligence like the one we seek to impose upon our world, but it is pure intelligence.

It is that intelligence that we are separated from in our efforts to become the creator ourselves. We have become so delighted in our own creations that we have lost our connection to that boundless, loving intelligence that is the basis of our lives.

Now the jury is out on how successful we have been in our efforts to become the creator. For all the genius behind our iPads, our smartphones and the software they run, not one of them has come close to expressing anything even resembling love, compassion, gratitude or joy. Not one of them has come close to creating in us anything that comes close to the feeling of joy when we see life itself expressed as nature, as a beautiful sunset, or a lightning storm, or the smile of a baby or the play of a puppy.

The Buddha spoke of a heavenly realm in which beings delighted in their own creations and the creations of others. It is in truth one of the higher heavenly realms. Below it are the realms in which beings delight in virtue and love, and the beauty of nature and creation itself, where they lack the vanity to become intoxicated with themselves and still appreciate what they are blessed to be a part of.

Each time I gaze upon the heavenly worlds and their display, they are all, without exception, beautiful beyond words. All of them, that is, except one. The highest one, beyond which is only Brahma.

When first I beheld it I was also left in awe, but not out of wonder, rather out of shock. For that realm, the highest of realms, where beings come close to being able to express themselves perfectly, that realm was a barren and desolate place. It was a wasteland. It took me many years to console myself from the experience of witnessing it. Where I had expected to behold the pinnacle of wonder and beauty, instead I found nothing but a barren wasteland. So intoxicated with themselves had these beings become that they had cut themselves off from the very source that sustained them and consumed the very ground that their existence depended upon. Gradually they had become obsessed with themselves and had lost their lustre and ceased to be, leaving behind them nothing but desolation.

So I suggest we forget all our ideas about some kind of personal achievement or enlightenment. I suggest we get over our vanity as soon as we possibly can. The world could do without creators such as us, but we most certainly could not do without it. Perhaps instead of becoming intoxicated with ourselves, we might come to understand or perhaps start to reflect upon what might be there, in the background, holding us while we flounder around delighting in ourselves. Because life itself does not, when it is left alone, degenerate into chaos. Far from it, it flourishes.

It degenerates when it is interfered with, but when left to express itself naturally, it organises itself into a state of balance. And it does not need us controlling it or managing it. We humans are the interference. Our intelligent human minds that we are so proud of, with all our great ideas about ourselves, we are what is in the way of something that is so perfect. The opportunity to be alive is the opportunity to turn up and witness what it is to be a part of it. That is the reason for our coming into being. To realise this is the longing that sits in the heart of every single one of us as the deepest of longings, and to come to the conclusion that life is just suffering would be a shame. If it is suffering, it is because we make it so.

On a beautiful morning right after dawn you might be able to feel that sublime consciousness of which I speak, very close to you. All too often these days we have crowded it out. But try to learn to recognise it when you are close to it. And when you recognise it, learn to rest in it, because when you do, it will become your teacher.

The conclusion that I have come to is not that life is just suffering, but that there is only love and not knowing it. That is all you will see going on everywhere, if you really pay attention: expressions of love or expressions of not knowing it. When the Buddha spoke of ignorance as the start of the causal chain from which arises greed, anger, ill-will and the mass of suffering that follows, what he meant was this; it is by not knowing love that beings bring themselves to suffering, and by coming to know love that they free themselves.

# CHAPTER EIGHTEEN

# THE WISH-FULFILLING JEWEL

To make peace with ourselves is the greatest gift we could have in this life. There is no material reward that has as great a value as the reward of being deeply at peace with who we are. Accepting who we are and accepting others as they are is the same thing. Behind our aversion, behind our ill-will, behind our greed, craving and attachment, there is always pride.

This constant comparing of my experience with how I think it should be as better, same or worse, and the constant comparing of myself with my ideas of who I think I am as better, same or worse, is pride and it is at the root of all suffering.

Quite often it is the last aspect of the ego that we see clearly. We identify where there is craving and greed, we identify where there is aversion and anger, but we do not necessarily spot how fixated upon ourselves we have become. We spot our greed but most often we cannot let it go because of pride. We spot our aversion but cannot let it go because of pride. It is the idea of ourself, who we think we are, that stands between us and making peace with who we actually are. It is our idea of ourself, what we think the world is, who we think others are, that maintains that sense of separation.

Of all the things that are clung to, the most doggedly clung to is the idea of me. And it is this idea of me that separates me from the experience I am actually having.

When you are looking to dismantle the three roots of suffering — ignorance, greed and aversion — understand that aversion and greed are not innate, they are conditioned states. And they are conditioned by ignorance. Ignorance is not paying attention, not seeing what is, as it is. The greatest ignorance of all is failing to recognise that this idea of ourselves is a totally illusory, dreamed-up and imagined idea of who I think I am. It is not until we dismantle this, that we enter truly into the experience we are having, as it is, and start to see it for what it is.

It is not when we complete our idea of ourself, but when we let it go, that we start to wake up to how it is. It is an act of generosity of spirit to surrender our fixation upon ourselves and allow things, ourselves and others, to be as they are.

To surrender the ego and its personal will to a deeper intelligence that is not in conflict takes courage and humility. It is not easy to do, but once you have seen for yourself the direction in which to go, never give up. If you have not enjoyed the quality of your mind in this life, and how your ideas of self have made life difficult, then work at it. Work at it.

There is an intelligence in the workings of this path out of suffering. To be alive is to stand upon that path, and, as I have said, the direction in which we head is entirely in our own hands. There is an intelligence in the whole universe, and when you look out there at all the myriad ways in which life expresses itself and how human beings express themselves, you will see only one of two things in the background behind the appearances you behold. You will either see love as the ground for the freedom from suffering, or not knowing love as the confusion that is the cause of the appearance of that suffering. When we see that, really see it, how can we have anything but compassion and love for one who, in confusion, does not see what is actually going on here?

So let us not get lost sitting round the dinner table arguing with each other about the nature of reality. Open your heart to the idea that we have not figured it all out yet, and perhaps that our faith in life is as important as our understanding of it. For every scientist who will tell you there is no divine principle at work in life because they have not yet managed to prove it, you will find far more beings who have taken the time to polish the lens of their mind so that they can see. I have not yet read the testimony of any one of them telling us that this life is a dry and mechanical process devoid of any higher purpose. It cannot be a coincidence that almost everyone who has taken the time to learn to see beyond the appearance of things has come back moved beyond words by what they have beheld. If we are no longer deeply in awe of life, it can only be because we have stopped paying attention to what is really going on here.

Perhaps we have stopped paying attention to what is going on around us every day because we are so busy paying attention to ourselves. What remains when our ideas and perception of self do fade away is a unity, a single process expressing itself exquisitely, creatively and imaginatively, everywhere. If you think your iPad is a genius creation then I suggest you stop, now and then, and look out at nature and what it is creating endlessly and everywhere, without leaving behind the slightest mess.

When we stop being intoxicated with ourselves and our creations, we awaken to the truth that we are a part of the same single process that everything that comes into being is a part of. As we come to rest within that process, we experience for the first time what it is to be free from conflict, what it is to be held. And in that moment there is no remaining sense of anything lacking.

This is the experience that we call the Wish-Fulfilling Jewel. Because it transforms what we thought were our desires into what really is our desire, and always has been our heart's deepest longing, which was to know for ourselves and come to understand what it is that is going on here, what we are a part of. When we realise for ourselves that our deepest longing has been fulfilled, we will know, as the Buddha said, 'That for which I have come here to do has been done by me.' Whatever willingness to harm ourselves or others in the pursuit of our desires there may have been will be gone and in its wake will be a deep conviction to honour and cherish life at every level as sacred.

So it is not about sitting on your cushion forty minutes a day meditating or practising mindfulness. It is not about seeing how long you can watch your breath, or feel inside your body or feel your gall bladder and your spleen, or tuning into the stillness of the room, and all of those things. It is about this coming home. It is about making that return journey to the basic ground of your being, and ending your sense of separation from what is around you.

So the point is this: be intelligent, but open your heart to the experience you are having and let it be your teacher, and stop trying to figure it all out in your mind. Live your life intelligently and look to your life as the ground upon which to sow the seeds for your future welfare, not just in this life but well beyond this. If you are concerned about the world we are going to leave behind for our children, then know it is and always will be a reflection of the choices we make about how to live.

It is not good enough to point the finger of blame at others, any more than it is to point it at ourselves. As Jesus said, we just do not know what we are doing. But when you do, when you understand, be willing to change as completely and unconditionally as you have to in order to become part of the solution and no longer the problem. It is not enough to say, 'I won't make a difference'. You will. If everyone waits for everyone else to change, we really are stuck.

We create our own suffering and we create our own way out of suffering. Nobody does it for us. Every liberated being, every single one who freed themselves from suffering did it by finding the courage to change, and overcoming the vanity of worrying about what others might think. The work that you have to do is the same work that every single one of us has to do, and we have to do it for ourselves. The Buddha did not bring anyone out of suffering and nor did Jesus. They simply pointed the way, and encouraged us to live consciously and considerately in such a way as to safeguard our welfare and the welfare of others, now and in the future.

So try to create the space in your life, so that when you get to the end of it you will know that what had to be done by you, for your welfare and the end of your suffering, has been done. Because that much you free yourself, that is also a step towards the freeing of others. Be willing to be the first to change and do not live like sheep, unwilling to take the first step until you know everyone else is coming with you.

Reflect upon the five precepts of conduct and see how fully you can commit to them. Make a list of the ten pārāmis and review them regularly. Stick them on your fridge or stick them next to the mirror where you brush your teeth in the morning, and just look at them, and ask yourself regularly, 'OK, how's it going?' And when you are finding life a bit tough, instead of thinking, 'Oh dear, it's all getting on top of me', ask yourself, 'What can I learn here?'

And if you look down the list and think about the challenge you are facing, you will find some inspiration to keep working at it. It is going to take more than a little patience, generosity or determination. But by the time you have found these ten qualities within you, you will be most of the way home.

This is the heart-essence of the Dharma. It is not packaged up in bite-sized chunks so you can practise it in ten minutes on the bus to work in the morning. I know it may not be convenient. But it is the Dharma that points the way. And the way that it points to is the cessation of suffering.

I do not always teach the Dharma as directly as this, and for many years I remodelled it for a modern western audience because I realised that actually people were interested in learning meditation for many reasons. They were not necessarily seeking the cessation of suffering. They were coming for some guidance in daily life and that is fair enough. So I started teaching the basis for a harmonious life and a harmonious mind. I realise that this rare and wonderful life we have is something to be lived as fully as we can, and that something that might help us get the most out of it, would be a great help.

I struggled with this for some years. My first teacher taught me how to teach meditation to a lay audience, for a healthy life in the here and now. My second teacher taught the path out of suffering to its end. When I left him to come back home to teach, explaining that I had to offer a Dharma for householders, not monks and nuns, he shed a tear, saying

'Life is brief. It is unsure. We should work for the cessation of suffering at every opportunity we can, and we should help to point that way to others.'

There is of course merit in both standpoints. Perhaps you will not mind if I explain it like this. There are many kinds of heavenly realms, more exalted than ours. Some are inhabited simply by those whose virtue is intact and, to growing degrees, who delight in the pleasurable but harmless things we delight in, like nature, visual beauty and sounds. Beyond these purely pleasurable realms are those of ever increasing states of peace and serenity where the beings who inhabit them are of ever purer and more subtle minds. Some have purified their minds through insight, others have upheld their innate purity and not lost it. Their ability to enter into, appreciate and enjoy any experience, from the ordinary to the sublime, is a reflection of the purity of their mind in that moment.

Some of these pure beings practise samatha (serenity) meditation. Others practise vipassanā (insight). The samatha devas have never seen eye to eye with the vipassanā devas. There is a debate that has gone on for a very long time. The samatha devas and the vipassanā devas are almost at loggerheads with each other. The Buddha looked out upon the world with the eye of wisdom and reflected, 'I must teach this Dharma for the welfare of beings and the way out of suffering.' He was concerned with the tremendous capacity we have to bring ourselves to suffering. He taught what he taught out of compassion.

Now the samatha devas, of which Brahma is one of the most exalted, looked down at the world, at me and people like me who were teaching Dharma to a fortunate audience like you, and said, 'Now come on. Hold on a minute. This is an awesome, extraordinary, profoundly beautiful universe and world that we are a part of. Why are you teaching the path out of suffering? Teach them how to love and how to live a life of love.'

This was the conclusion I myself came to, and so I started out teaching the path as the way to realise our full potential as beings.

And then there came a point when the vipassanā devas became concerned and said: 'Hold on a minute. This path of delight in the sacred is practised by those samatha devas up there in the heavenly realms. They are delighting in their good fortune because they kept their virtue. Their minds are taintless. They have not harmed another being along the way and there is no trace of selfishness in them. That is why they are delighting and revelling in their good fortune. Are you sure that the virtue of human beings is strong enough to show sufficient restraint that when, given everything they could ever dream of, they would not consume the planet that their life depends upon?'

So there it is, it is a very, very profound debate. Here we are in this extraordinary situation that takes eons to come about and that beings long to experience for goodness knows how long. And by failing to recognise what it is and honour it, the danger of bringing ourselves to suffering, rather than living it as an act of devotion, respect and gratitude, is great indeed.

This is basically the point. Here is the Dharma that teaches you how to live well and get the most out of your life, and the same Dharma that will show you the way to the causal cessation of suffering. The samatha devas live in hope that we as human beings can likewise keep our virtue, and live life as an expression of love without being a burden to others and the planet that we live on. And the vipassanā devas are saying, 'Look, the danger of beings bringing themselves to suffering is too great.'

I have grappled with this since I started teaching. Each time I teach I have to reflect on the audience that I am speaking to? What are their needs? I would love to teach that path of samatha so you could realise what your mind was truly capable of, but right now I do not think it is the time.

So this is the path that, if you follow it, will remove and dig out at the root the things that bring you to suffering. And I think that in all honesty it is for your welfare first and foremost, but also for everyone's welfare. I still sit on the fence, I have to be honest, but this is what the Buddha taught twenty-five centuries ago. He cared so deeply about the welfare of us humans that he implored us to free ourselves from suffering rather than simply revelling in our good fortune. He was well aware of how quickly such good fortune can come to an end if it is not honoured with the utmost integrity.

So when we as humans delight more in the pursuit of pleasure than the upholding of our virtue, dancing our life is not without risk. When we are willing to let go our unwillingness to harm ourselves or others in the pursuit of our desires, it is only a matter of time before we undo ourselves and the world we depend upon. That is the reason the Buddha taught what he did. He saw that our eyes are clouded with so much dust that we turn towards our desires, our sensual desires more consistently and more strongly than to our heart's true longing. When beings turn towards their heart's deepest longing, and their life stands upon that ground of harmlessness, then they can be taught how to truly dance.

Most of us in the west are of strong intellect but little faith. It is a shame. I have been teaching meditation now for over twenty years and I can tell you that, without fail, people are moved far more by the experience of being touched or getting close to what they might consider to be sacred in their lives, than they are by whatever insight arises in them from their practice. There are those of strong faith who just know or believe deeply, or perhaps have simply not forgotten that there is a profound goodness behind life, and whose hearts are filled with devotion to that. Such beings walk the devotional path, and through humility and gentleness free themselves of suffering far more quickly than those of us who have fallen in love with our own creations.

Of course it takes more than just faith to come into alignment with what we might call divine. It is our willingness to open towards something that is beyond our understanding that gets us in touch with that part of us that is pure, long before we really understand where it might come from. This path takes not only virtue but tremendous humility.

In a world where we are so focused upon the display of things, and in particular our own creations, there is little turning of our consciousness upwards to something higher than ourselves. Instead, we are folding in upon ourselves with self-absorption. Today we take far more photos of ourselves than of others, and certainly more than we take of the world around us. The way we avert our attention these days is rarely towards the purification of our heart and the realising of the essence of what we are. It is towards the gratification of what we perceive ourselves to be.

The path each of us chooses in life is very personal. The process of life, as I said, is not. Nobody is judged, there is no judging, there is nothing judging. There is just an intelligence by which this life functions, and you are either living in honour of it or not. And that is all there is to it. The world always has been and always will be a reflection of the consciousness of those upon it.

It is an extraordinary world that you are a part of, it really is. It is an amazing thing. And it has rolled with this extraordinary rhythm of intelligence down through the ages.

Sometimes it is as simple as turning your heart towards even the idea of what a taintless mind or being would be, a mind that is free of all selfish desire, free of any trace of willingness to harm or capacity to do so, a mind that arises with nothing but boundless love, compassion and appreciative joy, and being moved simply by that. It is important to know that there are such beings as this, and that the path that was walked by the Buddha has been walked by countless beings, and in time it can be walked by us.

How bright is your mind, as you wander on from this life, will be a reflection of how bright you have made it while you are here; which means keeping it dust-free the best you can. It is not enough to fall prey to sloth and torpor and say, 'Well you know what, it's all a little bit like hard work.'

It is hard work. It is hard work, but your investment in this life, in getting to this point, was huge. Make sure you invest during this life for whatever happens next. Remember the game of snakes and ladders. The longest snake is always one step before the finish line. You will never again come to a life as fortunate as this, so make it count. I am not saying this because I want to alarm you, I just want you to get what is really going on here. There are beings shedding tears of compassion for us all in our confusion, who long for us to be happy. But they cannot free us.

A prisoner when he is let out of jail is not free until he frees himself. So do not wait for things to change around you. Start to change yourself now, from the inside out, and take care of the quality of your mind, because it is your only real possession. If your heart has started to delight and open and love other people, and care deeply about others, just as much or even more than you would care about yourself, keep opening it. And do not stop until you are deeply and absolutely in awe of this life and feel so unfathomably grateful, endlessly so, because when that starts to happen to you, your mind is bright and brilliant, and that is the mind of these beautiful beings that we all long to feel close to. They are not dusty, they are not messy; they are beautiful, and if that is where you want to get to, then do what you need to do to make your own mind beautiful too. There are many miserable folk draped in the finest of robes, and many whose hearts fly free, whom no one would ever notice were even there. Remember that your real needs are few and more easily provided than you might think once you start to let go the things that do not serve your genuine welfare.

Whatever else it is that you might think you want to experience, there is nothing that you long to experience more than a spotless, taintless, boundless, unwavering, unshakeable peace within you, from which you could truly delight in the simple process of being alive. So be willing to give up what you do not need, or give it to those who do.

Whatever unwillingness to let go there still might be, keep working at it and never give up. Because I know that if you do one day come to glimpse for yourself the source of what I speak of here, there will be no wavering in your conviction to be close to it. This world is such an extraordinary, rare occurrence. To come to a fortunate human life is an even more rare occurrence. Once upon a time you longed to appear here, you longed to turn up, to experience what it is to come into being in material form. And it was enough, it is enough, only to enter into the creative process itself. To wake up to what it is that you are a part of is enough. But somehow, somewhere along the line, we have become so intoxicated with the idea of ourselves as the creator that we have bent this world to our will and lost our connection to the creative principle that is actually governing our lives. This life is not governed by the will of man and to bend it to our will does not come without a cost. The more we bend it, the greater becomes that cost. For nothing in nature can remain out of balance indefinitely, and ultimately this world is governed by natural laws infinitely more powerful than our will.

I remember one morning, sitting with one of my teachers, and he said to me, 'These spiritual teachings, the flourishing of these spiritual teachings, it's just like a match. It will blaze brightly only for a while. But if you want to make a fire burn for a long time you need to create a heart to it.' That heart is not built on knowledge alone. It is built on conduct and choices. We are all going to have to make choices. We are those people that the Buddha spoke of who have little dust in their eyes. We have to work this out. And we cannot expect to wait until we are shown the way or told what to do. Because if we cannot work it out with all our intelligence and our capacity to recognise these things at work within us, then who will?

What my teacher said about the match - do not let it be a match that burns brightly within in you, inspires you and then quite quickly burns out and just sits in the background of your life as an unanswered longing or sadness. You need to put fuel on your fire, and you need to tend it, and when it has a heart then it will burn continuously and it will always show you the way. You give it a little fuel, blow on it occasionally and it will blaze for you. But you need to put the foundations down so that it has a heart. It is not just about receiving these teachings. It is about imbibing their essence, putting them into practice and living by them, so that, one day in the future, you might come to truly delight in being alive in a time when consciousness is flourishing and not on the wane. It is that for which all of us have come here. It is in our hands which way we go. Whether you feel you were born in the light or born in the darkness does not matter. What matters is the direction in which you walk.

At the age of 80, after having taught Dharma for forty-five years, the Buddha was nearing the end of his life. In the moments before his final passing away he was approached by those most close to him and asked for his final piece of advice to them all.

He pointed towards the shady groves, the quiet places where nature is undisturbed and the heart could rest peacefully immersed in the way of things and said:

'Go forth and meditate lest you regret it later. Decay is inherent in all compound things. Work out your own salvation with diligence.'

While the light is still shining in your heart, while you are still able to pay heed to its calling and recognise the way home for yourself, now is the time to do what has to be done by each of you, for your own well-being and the well-being of those around you. As the Buddha said, 'Do it now, lest you regret it later.'

*Araham SammāsamBuddho Bhagavā*
*Buddham Bhagavāntam Abhivādemi*

Burgs continues to teach meditation and chi kung
around the UK.

For more information on the healing meditation
or Dharma as discussed in this book, please visit his website at
www.theartofmeditation.org

For all correspondence please email Burgs at
**enquiries@theartofmeditation.org**

Printed in Great Britain
by Amazon

37602466R00130